The MYSTERY OF THE AGES

John W. Rush, BTh, MTS

WESTBOW
PRESS*
A DIVISION OF THOMAS NELSON
& ZONDERVAN

WestBow Press books may be ordered through booksellers or by contacting:

WestBow Press
A Division of Thomas Nelson & Zondervan
1663 Liberty Drive
Bloomington, IN 47403
www.westbowpress.com
844-714-3454

ISBN: 979-8-3850-2166-6 (sc)
ISBN: 979-8-3850-2168-0 (hc)
ISBN: 979-8-3850-2167-3 (e)

Print information available on the last page.

WestBow Press rev. date: 03/13/2024

Contents

Contents

Introduction

The text on which this book is based is found in Colossians 1:24–29 (underlined emphasis mine).

I now rejoice in my sufferings for you, and fill up in my flesh what is lacking in the afflictions of Christ, for the sake of His body, which is the church,

Of which I became a minister according to the stewardship from God which was given me for you, to fulfill the word of God,

The mystery which has been hidden from ages and from generations, but now has been revealed in His saints.

To them God willed to make known what are the riches of the glory of this mystery among the Gentiles: which is <u>Christ in you, the hope of glory</u>.

Him we preach, warning every man and teaching every man in all wisdom, that we may present every man perfect (mature) in Christ Jesus.

To this end I also labor, striving according to His working which works in me mightily.

The chapters that follow will dissect this concept item by item, culminating in the supernatural ministry of the Holy Spirit within the heart of every believer. What is He seeking to accomplish, and how does He go about producing this desired end and purpose in the lives of His saints?

Each chapter will also include a true story about the transformation of many lives over the years of ministry. The stories are true, but the names have been changed to respect the individuals' privacy. Lest we appear to be focusing on the church, the people, or the author of this book, each chapter will illustrate the transformation of people through the touch of the Master's hand.

Many years ago, I came across the poem written by Myra Brooks Welch titled "The Touch of the Master's Hand." From the first time I read it, and through many decades of ministry, this poem has been a source of great blessing and encouragement. May the Lord bless you with it as well!

Special Notes

1. Each chapter opens with a true story under the heading of "The Master's Touch." These accounts are chosen to illustrate the gracious power of the Lord in our lives and in the ministry of evangelism! Jesus is the Master and can transform a sinner into a saint in a split second!
2. The names in these stories have all been removed for the protection and privacy of the people involved.
3. Each scripture quoted in this book is from the New King James Version.
4. The quotations used in this book are credited in footnotes except for those that have become public domain through the years.
5. Certain key influential people in my book are identified with their real names. In some cases, these highly respected leaders have gone home to glory.
6. "The Touch of the Master's Hand" by Myra Brooks Welch, as quoted next, is used as a theme throughout the book to introduce the wonderful grace of Jesus.

"The Touch of the Master's Hand"

BY
MYRA BROOKS WELCH

T'was battered and scarred, and the auctioneer thought it scarcely worth his while to waste much time on the old violin, but he held it up with a smile;

"What am I bidden good folks," he cried, "Who'll start the bidding for me?" "A dollar, a dollar; then two!" "Only two? Two dollars, and who'll make it three? Three dollars once; three dollars twice; going for three …" But no, from the room far back a grey-haired man came forward and picked up the bow; then wiping the dust from the old violin, and tightening the loosened strings, he played a melody pure and sweet as a caroling angel sings.

The music ceased, and the auctioneer, with a voice that was quiet and low, said: "What am I bid for the old violin?" and he held it up with the bow. "A thousand dollars, and who'll make it two? Two thousand! And who'll make it three? Three thousand once, three thousand twice, and going, and gone," said he.

The people cheered, but some of them cried, "We do not quite understand what changed its worth."

Swift came the reply: "The touch of the master's hand!"

"And many a man with life out of tune, and battered and scarred with sin, is auctioned cheap to the thoughtless crowd, much like the old violin. A mess of pottage, a glass of wine, a game—and he travels on. "He is going once … and going twice … he is going and almost gone!" But the Master comes, and the foolish crowd can never quite understand the worth of a soul, and the change that's wrought by the touch of the Master's hand!

May the Lord bless you as you pursue this journey with me.

A Personal Testimony

During my ministry as the senior pastor of a Baptist church north of Toronto, we experienced an internal conflict over the question of the charismatic movement. My board of deacons urged me to preach a series of messages on the doctrine of the Holy Spirit in an attempt to settle these issues.

Very shortly after that meeting with the deacons, I began a series of five or six messages on what the Bible teaches about the ministry of the Holy Spirit. It was quite successful in clarifying our position and in stifling the arguments among the people—with two remarkable exceptions.

Two ladies, independently of each other, left the church in anger. One declared, "The pastor does not believe in the Holy Spirit," and she transferred to a charismatic assembly in town. The other was fully persuaded that Pastor Rush had become a charismatic and should step down from the role of senior pastor. She left to join a legalistic assembly!

This testimony is a somewhat optimistic attempt to forestall this kind of confusion, if such a thing is even possible!

First of all, let me state clearly that I am not a Pentecostal, charismatic, or vineyard believer.

I love my brothers and sisters who are of that persuasion for their zeal, their evangelistic fervor, and their freedom in worship. I part company with them in the area of biblical exegesis and maintain that the authority for our faith rests in the objective revelation of truth found only in the Bible. The subjective realm of experience must submit itself to the clear teaching of God's Word.

On the other hand, I strongly believe that the fundamental churches of today in our Western world have a desperate need for a spiritual revival and to discover the power and joy of a Spirit-filled life. I pastored a Bible-preaching church for three years before discovering the filling of the Holy Spirit. This testimony is an attempt to illustrate what this wonderful experience meant in my life and ministry.

My first pastorate was the product of a summer field assignment following my second year of seminary training. During the balance of my seminary training in Toronto, I traveled down to Leamington (about a four-hour trip) and conducted the services on Sundays.

Following graduation, Ann and I were married and settled in a rental house in Leamington. We both had to find other jobs to supplement the meager salary provided by the church.

We were able, however, to purchase the beautiful church building on Elliott Street owned by the Mennonite Brethren Church. Its seating capacity was about 250 people. We had twenty-seven.

I struggled with a sense of futility and failure, wondering what was missing in my ministry. I became convinced that I should seek the Lord and search the scriptures for an answer.

I asked Ann to cancel or reschedule all of my appointments for the next week so that I could be alone with the Lord in my office. With this arrangement in place, I began a serious search of the issues involved with the Spirit-filled life.

I read all of the material that I had collected from the Pentecostal and charismatic writers, prepared to accept their position on the "second blessing" or "baptism of the Holy Spirit." I compared their claims and conclusions to the New Testament passages dealing with the subject and found them wanting. It is easy to make claims based on personal experience and then find "proof texts" in the Bible to support them. In my heart, I knew that this position was seriously flawed.

Next I tackled the writings of the fundamental scholars that I had studied and respected over the years. Many of these men of God seemed to draw very close to the issue but left me wondering what was missing! I wondered if the charismatics were right after all! I also wondered why my seminary training had omitted a biblical explanation of this vital subject. Oh yes, we had studied Arthur W. Pink on the Holy Spirit, but we failed to have any frank and open discussions about living Spirit-filled lives, having the anointing of the Spirit on our ministries, or preaching with the Spirit's unction!

At the breakfast table on Thursday morning, Ann asked if I could take a break from my search and drive into Windsor for supplies from the Christian bookstore. I was happy to have the change of pace and felt that the Lord had a reason for this short trip at that particular time.

While Ann was selecting her Sunday school supplies, I wandered around the store, browsing through their books and pamphlets. As I approached the checkout at the front, my eye caught the title of a small booklet. Then I was astounded to see that the author was William Graham Scroggie, whom I had studied in seminary and held in very high regard. The title was *Be Filled with the Spirit,* and the cost was twenty-five cents! I snatched it up and added it to Ann's purchases.

I could hardly wait to get back to my study at the church and see what Scroggie had to say on this immensely vital subject. I must have read through the booklet about three or four times before I found myself on my knees at the side of my desk.

Scroggie's logic was impeccable. He pointed out that we received the wonderful gift of eternal life from the Second Person of the Godhead when we humbled ourselves and asked Him for it in simple faith like a child would have. He pondered why we would complicate the need for the Third Person of the Godhead to take control of our lives and fill us! Why don't we humble ourselves and ask Him to fill us in simple childlike faith and repentance of sin? He then suggested that we get up off our knees and live as Spirit-filled believers.

As I prayed that afternoon, I confessed my sin of unbelief and pride in seeking to complicate what God had provided so simply for His children. I asked the Spirit of God to take over my life and ministry and to fill me with His presence and power. A great burden rolled away, and my heart was overwhelmed with joy inexpressible and full of glory (1 Peter 1:8). I stood up with a deep conviction that my ministry was now His ministry, and that frustration and folly had been replaced with filling and fruitfulness.

At no time was I prostrate on the floor in a trancelike condition. I did not experience any ecstatic gifts. In fact, my mind was clearer and sharper than it had been for quite some time, and I was overwhelmed by the sense of His presence, peace, pardon, and power in my heart.

On Sunday morning, my message was extremely easy to bring to the people gathered together—a larger attendance than we had been seeing week after week. I decided to give an altar call, and to my delight, one person came forward to receive Christ as Savior! It had been weeks since we had seen our last soul brought to a saving knowledge of Christ.

For the next few weeks, someone responded to the Gospel invitation each Sunday. Our numbers began to show marked signs of growth, and there was an atmosphere of excitement and enthusiasm among our people.

During this same period of change, we had an unexpected visit from a special family friend. Silas Fox was my father's lifelong best friend and had served the Lord very effectively as a missionary to India. He had heard of our new church plant and wanted to see how we were getting along. I took him for a tour of our new church facility and followed him from my study into the auditorium and down the sloping aisle toward the front. I had to stop very suddenly, because Silas had dropped to his knees, lifted his hands toward heaven, and raised his voice in prayer, praising God for His wonderful work in Leamington and saying that the pews would very soon be filled to overflowing! His prayer was heard and answered in the throne room of heaven!

At the request of a number of believers, we began to train them in the methods of Evangelism Explosion, with eventually about forty-five workers equipped in the ministry of leading souls to Christ. This became an important factor in the successful harvest that was experienced during the last three years of our stay there. During that time, our workers recorded over one thousand professions of faith in Jesus Christ, throughout the area, and as far away as the state of Michigan.

We became involved in outreach at the Leamington District Agricultural Fair by renting space on the arena floor and creating an attractive exhibit that caught people's attention. In our third year at the fair, we rented seventy-five linear feet on the arena floor right at the curve. This then fanned out into a wedge-shaped space that allowed us to create five counseling rooms and an office. The façade of the display included an alcove with artificial grass and flowers, white wrought-iron lawn furniture, and an arbor covered with flowers over the entrance into the counseling rooms. There were continuous colored slides of the Holy Land and a loop of instrumental Gospel music over our speaker system.

Our workers were divided into two shifts, covering the daytime and evening hours and rotating every other day. In those five days, 205 people prayed to receive Christ as Savior at our exhibit. We had drug addicts, prostitutes, gang members, and hardened criminals who came to faith in Jesus that week. Along with these, many ordinary residents of the town became Christians and sought baptism and church membership in the following weeks.

One Wednesday afternoon, I went into the church auditorium alone for a time of prayer and personal worship. I sat at the piano, played some of my favorite Gospel songs, and sang along from time to time. I suddenly sensed that I was not alone at all! I turned around and found a very good-looking young man sitting in the front pew with a look of blessing on his face. He apologized for intruding and then introduced himself to me.

He said, "My name is Daniel, and I am a new believer in Jesus. I am looking for a church home because the one that I now attend does not preach the Gospel. I am a singer and would like to serve the Lord with my voice."

I asked Daniel to sing for me, and I accompanied him on the piano. His wonderful rich baritone voice filled the auditorium easily. I thought that I was listening to George Beverly Shea! I asked Daniel if he would come to our church and sing before each of my morning messages. He was delighted to agree, and our church services took on a whole new richness and power.

As Daniel was singing his solo before my sermon one Sunday, I had a peculiar inner, silent discussion with the Holy Spirit. No audible words were spoken, but I had no doubt about the content of the interaction!

"Do you trust Me, John?" He asked. I replied that I most certainly did! Then He challenged me as I had never been challenged in the ministry before.

"Put away your notes, and let Me preach today!"

I thought that I was losing my mind! I thought that such a suggestion could never have come from the Lord! I looked at my seventeen pages of notes and found myself placing them on the pew beside me, just as Daniel finished his solo and sat down!

The next half hour was totally amazing to me! The Lord provided me with a New Testament passage, a clear outline, cross-references, illustrations, and applications. What struck me much more than this, however, was the power of God's Spirit in the message. It was visibly obvious that God was convicting many people throughout the auditorium of their personal sin and desperate need of Him!

When the altar call was given, they began to come in groups of three or four to the front. Many of them were weeping their way to the altar. The Lord said, "Count them!" The total number at the front that morning was twenty-seven, The Lord said, "It took you three years to reach twenty-seven people. I did it in thirty minutes! Will you let Me take control of this ministry?"

While this experience was amazing and powerful in my spiritual walk with God, it was the exception rather than the rule. On quite a few occasions through the many decades of ministry, I have been clearly prompted by the Holy Spirit to change my message at the last moment and preach from a text that He had brought to my attention. In every case, obedience to such prompting resulted in much blessing—for me personally and for the people in the congregation at the time.

The rule has always been the thorough preparation and research of material used in messages, but the constant blessing of being filled with the Spirit has been manifest in great liberty and unction. It has been wonderful to sense the power of God's Spirit at work in the hearts and minds of the many hundreds of people who have been brought to a saving knowledge of Jesus Christ!

The filling of the Spirit is not only an act, but it is, primarily, a process. In subsequent chapters of this book, we will be examining the biblical teaching on this important subject. The Lord led us to the pastorate in five Fellowship Baptist churches in Ontario and on two separate occasions with the Peoples Church in Toronto. More recently we served in Melbourne, Australia, broadcasting the Gospel under the auspices of HCJB Global. In all of these ministry opportunities, the power and blessing of the Holy Spirit have been very evident and enjoyed.

While in Australia, we had the privilege of broadcasting over 260 half-hour radio programs into the Asia-Pacific region via shortwave. During the last year and a half of our ministry there, we were privileged to travel throughout the five states of that great country, preaching the Gospel in a great number of churches. Without exception, the Spirit of God reaped a harvest of precious souls in those churches.

On one special occasion, I had the opportunity of preaching a Gospel message in our home church in Melbourne. At the altar call, about fourteen people responded with an upraised hand. Among them was a dignified white-haired gentleman who had retired from the ministry in England and moved to Australia with his wife to be with their family.

I offered those who had raised their hands a booklet that would further explain the importance of what they had done. I urged them all to come down to the front of the auditorium and I would give them this booklet personally. I looked up to see this retired minister approaching me with a great smile on his face. He said, "John, I have come for a booklet!"

I asked him to explain why he had made this commitment today, in light of his very admirable life of service to Jesus Christ. He replied, "Today I realized that my faith was only intellectual and that I needed to surrender my heart to Him!"

Later, at a farewell party that the church held for us before Ann and I returned to Toronto, I had a chance to chat with this gentleman. I asked, "Sir, has the commitment that you made to Christ several weeks ago made any difference to you?" He replied, "Oh my, yes! It has revolutionized my fellowship with God, my devotional reading of His word, and my ability to share my faith with strangers and friends! It has made all the difference in the world!"

It must never be concluded that the filling of the Holy Spirit has elevated us to a spiritual plane above the rest of our Christian friends! We still have our battles with the world, the flesh, and the devil. In fact, walking in the Spirit often increases Satan's desire to deflate you, discourage you, or deceive you into compromise with sin. The greatest arena of spiritual warfare lies between the ears and in the heart. Satan wants to influence your thinking, your attitudes, and your personal choices so that he can gain a toehold in your heart. He will even allow you to carry on a successful ministry if he can con you into a life of spiritual lethargy, complacency, and compromise! He knows what tactics will work most effectively on you and plots his schemes accordingly.

The only way to live a victorious Christian life is through surrender to the Lordship of Christ and a renewed filling of the Spirit on a continuous basis.

THE MASTER'S TOUCH

My mentor in the ministry, Dr. Lindsay Howan (senior pastor of Riverside Baptist Church, Windsor) helped me in the launch of a church plant in the town of Leamington, Ontario. We arranged for the rental of the Margaret D. Benny Public School for Sunday services to begin on the first week of August 1964.

One of the exercises that we shared was door-to-door visitation, distributing fliers that invited people to our first service on August 4. While making these calls on my side of the street, I knocked on the door of a home that seemed to be empty, without any lights visible on the inside. To my surprise, a good-looking, tall, young man came to the door. He introduced himself as Rob. I handed him a flier and said, "I'm Pastor John and would love to have you come to our first service on August 4!"

Rob invited me in and launched into about two hours of argumentation in favor of his agnostic persuasion. He asked me many questions that I had never heard before, and I was at a loss to reply with any intelligent information or logic!

I left Rob's house that day defeated and discouraged. I never wanted to do any door-to-door visitation again! In fact, I wanted to leave Leamington and cancel any proposed church services in the public school! Pastor Howan decided to get me away from the frustration so we went golfing! During the nine holes that we played that afternoon, Lindsay shared his own personal testimony of serving the Lord and meeting up with opposition, criticism, and inadequacy. We prayed together and went back to the visitation program the next day!

About three years later, our congregation was meeting in our own church building purchased from the Mennonite Brethren Assembly.

By now we were seeing a movement of the Holy Spirit in the town, and our numbers had grown significantly.

As the service began, I was blessed by the attendance of a large group of people sitting together in the second or third pew in the center of the auditorium. Afterward I was standing at the doorway out from the auditorium shaking hands and chatting with new people. A young man came to me and said, "You don't know who I am, do you?"

My reply was that I recognized his face but could not remember his name. He said, "You visited me at my family's home three years ago, and I tried very hard to challenge your faith in God with a lot of questions. You weren't able to answer them, but I wasn't able to destroy your faith. After you had gone, I asked my dad if I could borrow his Bible, and I began to search through the New Testament to see if it made any sense. After reading many pages of the New Testament, I asked Jesus to come into my life and show me the truth."

After his own conversion, he was instrumental in leading his mother, father, brother, and sister to faith in the Master who had put a new song in his heart!

PART 1

Chapter One

MYSTERY DEFINED

The word *mystery* comes from the Latin *mysterium* and from the Greek *musterion* (plural: *musteria*). Our English word means "something that is difficult or impossible to explain."[1]

In the first generation of the church, society was plagued with "mystery religions" that were sects of existing religions and sprang out of them when those religions became corrupted and lax in the performance of their religious rules and regulations. Mystery religions would arise from them in an attempt to redeem the depravity and disintegration of the official system.

In these mystery religions, only those who were initiated into the cult would be able to understand the hidden message or hidden agenda of the group. The leaders would impart something of the hidden secret or agenda to the initiates as they were granted full membership into the sect. They were then sworn to secrecy and forbidden to share this information with anyone outside of the circle of knowledge. In some cases, the revelation was progressive: imparted to the initiates in a series of steps or stages, each requiring further allegiance and commitment on the part of the initiate.

---

[1] *Compact Oxford English Dictionary*, 672.

One ancient form of a mystery religion predated the New Testament age. It was the Mystery Religion of Hermes in Greece. Hermes was the Greek god of boundaries and the travelers who crossed them; of shepherd and cowherds; of thieves and road travelers; of orators and wit; of literature and poets; of athletics; of weights and measures; of invention; of general commerce; and of the cunning of thieves and liars! To the Romans, he was known as Mercury and was generally thought to carry too big a portfolio!

A MODERN MYSTERY RELIGION

A modern form of a mystery religion is found in the hidden teachings of the Masonic Lodge! The tragedy of the Masonic Lodge is that you can progress up through all of the degrees—even up to the thirty-third degree—and still be in the dark concerning the satanic nature of the organization! How is such a thing possible?

The secret behind the mystery religion called Masons is that they have two complete organizations in one system! The visible order shows itself as a fraternal brotherhood dedicated to the betterment of society in general and in their fraternal brothers in particular.

The *Scottish Rite Journal* described Manley P. Hall as "Masonry's greatest philosopher in 1990." About him they wrote, "The world is a far better place because of Manley Palmer Hall, and we are better persons for having known him and his work."

In *Lectures on Ancient Philosophy*, Manly Hall wrote,

> Freemasonry is a fraternity within a fraternity—an
> outer organization concealing an inner brotherhood
> of the elect—it is necessary to establish the existence
> of these two separate and yet interdependent orders,

the one visible, the other invisible. The visible society is a splendid camaraderie of the "free and accepted" men enjoined to devote themselves to ethical, educational, fraternal, patriotic, and humanitarian concerns. The invisible society is a secret and most august (defined as "of majestic dignity, grandeur") fraternity whose members are dedicated to the service of a mysterious arcannum arcandrum (defined as "most secret, a mystery").[2]

Hall explained the secret power behind the Masons in a book titled *The Lost Keys of Freemasonry.* He declared,

> When a Mason learns the key to the warrior on the block is the proper application of the dynamo of living power, he has learned the mystery of his craft. The seething energies of Lucifer are in his hands and before he may step onward and upward, he must prove his ability to properly apply energy.[3]

Obviously, millions of people have been duped into thinking that there is nothing wrong with being a member of the Freemasons! In actual fact, a strategy exists within this organization to cover up the dark side to those who have expressed their allegiance to Jesus Christ. They are given the official position, which is the product of deceit and falsehood. It has been estimated that 95 percent of all Masons are totally unaware of the inner circle secret cadre.

In his book *Morals and Dogma,* Albert Pike writes,

> Masonry, like all religions, all the Mysteries, Hermeticism, and Alchemy, conceals its secrets

---

[2] Manly Palmer Hall, *Lectures on Ancient Philosophy,* 397.
[3] Manly Palmer Hall, *The Lost Keys of Freemasonry,* chapter 3.

from all except the Adepts and Sages, or the Elect, and uses false explanations and misrepresentations of its symbols to mislead those who deserve only to be misled; to conceal the Truth, which it calls Light, and take them away from it.[4]

NEW TESTAMENT MYSTERIES

The New Testament's use of the term *mystery* was much different from that found among the ancient mystery religions or today's Freemasons.

While the word *musterion* occurs twenty-seven times in the New Testament, there are twelve specific subjects that make use of the Greek word *musterion*. In each case, the biblical writers had a precise definition in mind.

Dr. H. L. Wilmington provides us with this definition: "A mystery in the Bible is a previously hidden truth, not revealed in the Old Testament, but declared, and at times, explained in the New Testament."[5]

The twelve New Testament mysteries are outlined below:

1. **The Mystery of the Kingdom (Matthew 13:3–50; Mark 4:1–25; Luke 8:4–15)**

   Jesus presented His disciples with a series of eight parables recorded in the references cited above (especially in Matthew 13:3–50) in which He explained a significant fact about the prophecy of Zechariah (Zechariah 12:10; 14:8–9)

---

[4] Albert Pike, *Morals and Dogma*, 98.
[5] Dr. H. L. Wilmington, *Wilmington's Guide to the Bible*, 462.

concerning the kingdom of heaven. Unknown to the Old Testament believers, there would be a gap (lasting over two thousand years to date) between the time when Israel would pierce their Messiah and the time when they would mourn over Him. During that gap, the kingdom would take an internal form and would include the Gentile believers as well as the Jewish believers. The external form of that longed-for kingdom would take place at the Second Coming of Jesus Christ in power and great glory.

John MacArthur Jr. writes,

> The period between Christ's first and second comings has been called the parenthesis, the interim, the interregnum, and many other such terms. It is a period that was not revealed in the Old Testament, a period to which Jesus refers as "the mysteries of the kingdom."[6]

2. **The Mystery of the Rapture (1 Corinthians 15:51–52; 1 Thessalonians 4:16)**

While the Old Testament records two events that foreshadow the rapture of the church (Enoch, Genesis 5:24, and Elijah, 2 Kings 2:11), their sudden departures are not explained, nor is the concept clarified until the Holy Spirit revealed it to the apostles as they wrote the New Testament scriptures.

The doctrine of the resurrection of believers in glorified bodies was understood as early as the book of Job, one of the most ancient books in the Bible. Job declared, "For I know that my Redeemer lives, and He shall stand at last upon the earth; and after my skin is destroyed, this I know, that in my flesh I shall see God" (Job 19:25–26 NKJV).

---

[6] John MacArthur Jr., *The MacArthur New Testament Commentary,* 343.

Consistent exegesis of New Testament scriptures inevitably leads to the position of the premillennial pretribulation rapture of the church! The church is the physical embodiment of the Restrainer, the Holy Spirit (2 Thessalonians 2:7), and will be removed when He is taken out of the way. The ministry of the Holy Spirit will then continue for seven more years in the same manner as it had during the Old Testament days.

All of the biblical signs of the times will be fulfilled during the seven-year tribulation period. There are no signs given that precede the rapture of the church. The return of Christ for His chosen bride is imminent and could occur at any moment.

Paul encourages us that "we who are alive and remain shall be caught up together (raptured) with them (resurrected ones) in the clouds to meet the Lord in the air" (1 Thessalonians 4:17). He tells the Corinthian believers that during that rapture experience, we shall undergo a metamorphosis that will only take "the twinkling of an eye" (1 Corinthians 15:51–52).

3. **The Mystery of the Church as the Body of Christ (Romans 12:4–5; 1 Corinthians 12:12–13, 27; Ephesians 5:30; Colossians 1:18)**

The church is composed of all who have found a saving relationship with Jesus Christ. The church has been given the assignment of representing Christ to our world in each generation as the age of grace continues. In this imagery, we make up the body of Christ of which He is the Head.

This implies that we are to be in subjection to the Lordship of Christ, to live in unity and harmony with Him and each other, to labor for the Master in extending His kingdom to others, and to be fully in step with His values and priorities.

4. **The Mystery of the Church as the Bride of Christ (Ephesians 5:22–33)**

Verses 22–33 of the fifth chapter of Ephesians are often read as part of Christian wedding ceremonies, and rightly so because there are clear exhortations within this passage concerning the duties of wives to their husbands and of husbands to their wives. However, Paul points out that this is a word picture of our love relationship to Jesus Christ by faith. He is the Bridegroom, and we are His chosen bride. Other passages that affirm the truth of this comparison are 2 Corinthians 11:2, Ephesians 5:2, 3:14–21, and Revelation 21:9.

The bride will leave her father's house to join the Bridegroom as He approaches her earthly home. They, along with the entourage accompanying the Bridegroom, will return to His Father's house where He will present His bride for inspection (the Bema Seat) and approval (rewards). They will live together in the full blessing of the promises of the Bridegroom to the bride in their betrothal.

5. **The Mystery of the Indwelling Christ (Galatians 2:20; Colossians 1:26–27; 4:3; Romans 16:25–26)**

This fifth mystery is the subject and focus of this entire book, so we will only briefly comment on this wonderful truth. The "middle wall of partition" between the Jew and Gentile people was broken down through the blood shed on Calvary's cross (Ephesians 2:11–22). The "new man" referred to in this passage is not Jewish, as required in the

Old Testament. A Gentile would need to become a proselyte of Judaism in order to enter the Mosaic Covenant with Yahweh. Now the New Covenant demands that both Jew and Gentile become a "new man" through faith in Jesus Christ as Savior and Lord (see 2 Corinthians 5:17).

6. **The Mystery of the Incarnate Christ (Colossians 2:2, 9; 1 Corinthians 2:7)**

One of the main objections held by Moslems against Christianity is the incarnation of Jesus Christ. In Islam such a union between the Creator and the creature is totally unacceptable because of the sinfulness of man. If God were to become a man, He would no longer be holy and thus would cease to be God!

This is a perfectly logical point of view; however, it is built on a faulty premise. The basis of this conviction is that there is no possible way for God to enter His physical universe without becoming contaminated in the process.

The mystery of the incarnation rests on two significant truths.

First, the virgin birth of Jesus Christ was a miracle of God's creation. Mary became pregnant without having marital relations with her fiancé, Joseph. Furthermore, she was not unfaithful to him as he had feared but was chosen by God's grace to receive the creative touch of God's Holy Spirit so that a baby boy could be conceived without inheriting the curse of original sin through the blood of an earthly father.

In every way but two, Jesus was a normal human being. He had a sinless human nature and He had a perfect divine nature at the same time. Theologians refer to this as "the Hypostatic Union" of Jesus Christ.

It means that He was always entirely human (sin excepted), and He was always completely divine, in possession of all of His divine attributes, yet surrendering their independent use while He was in His body of humiliation (Philippians 2:5–8). This humbling of Himself is called the "kenosis" of Christ in which He laid aside His heavenly glory and subjected Himself to the challenges of humanity. Scripture teaches that He was tempted (Matthew 4:1–11; Hebrews 4:15; 7:26) in every way as we are, yet there was nothing in Him that would yield to that temptation. He came to destroy the works of the devil (1 John 3:8), and He alone can provide us with victory (Romans 8:37; 1 Corinthians 15:57; Romans 6:14; Ephesians 6:10–13; 1 John 5:4).

7. **The Mystery of Godliness (1 Timothy 3:16)**

This mystery is similar to the one that we have just considered, except that its focus is not quite the same. The "Mystery of Godliness" described by Paul here encompasses the whole eternal plan of redemption. God is essentially a Spirit that is invisible yet glorious. He inhabited eternity as Father, Son, and Holy Spirit, without the need of anything or anyone to complete Him or add anything to Him that was missing.

Nevertheless, He planned from before the creation of space, matter, and time that He would speak into existence our universe and would crown this creation with the master race of human beings, made in His own image (meaning His moral and spiritual nature, not our bodies). Those innocent human beings placed in a perfect environment would succumb to the evil temptation of a fallen angel named Lucifer and plunge the entire race into spiritual and eternal death.

The plan of redemption was already clear in God's omniscience that could only be possible if the human race was given a righteous and innocent substitute who would take upon Himself the guilt and shame of our depravity, paying the price demanded by God's perfect holiness, righteousness, and justice. Such a substitute had to be human but also had to be infinitely holy.

Only God Himself could become such a sacrifice for sin, but He could only make such a provision for our redemption in the Person of Jesus Christ, the Son of God and God the Son.

Our text declares that this mystery includes the following: God was manifest in the flesh; He was justified in the Spirit; He was seen of angels; He was preached among the Gentiles, believed on in the world, and received up into glory.

8. **The Mystery of Lawlessness (2 Thessalonians 2:3–12; Matthew 13:33)**

The expression "the mystery of lawlessness is already at work" (2 Thessalonians 2:7) reflects the spiritual warfare that has been underway since the fall in the Garden of Eden. John writes that this agenda of evil will increase in intensity and prevalence as the age progresses toward its climax, culminating in the revelation of the Antichrist whom Paul refers to as "the son of perdition" (2 Thessalonians 2:3).

There is a force within society that is holding back the tsunami of iniquity that would otherwise devastate all of society in one gigantic crashing surge. "The Restrainer" in 2 Thessalonians 2:7 is clearly the Holy Spirit; however, His ministry of restraint is largely conducted through the "salt and light" influence of the church of Jesus Christ! Since we are indwelt by the Holy Spirit, it follows that the church will be raptured when the Spirit's restraint is at an end. His ministry from that point on will revert back to what it was in the Old Testament days. He was external to the believers and came upon them to grant special wisdom and power for the challenge of that day.

9. **The Mystery of Israel's Present Blindness (Romans 11:25)**

Israel has always been blind to spiritual truth! The Old Testament history of God's covenant people is tragic and sordid in the extreme. It wasn't until God placed them in seventy years of the Babylonian captivity that they finally were delivered from their sinful attraction to idolatry! The message of the prophets to Israel was one of constant condemnation for their "spiritual adultery." In fact Isaiah referred to them as Sodom and Gomorrah in the first chapter of his prophecy, and Jeremiah consistently warned them that the wrath of God was about to be poured out on His own people. They would suffer death by pestilence, drought, and the sword, and only a remnant would be carried away captive by Nebuchadnezzar.

While some feel that Israel was punished with blindness because they rejected Jesus Christ as their Messiah, Paul makes it clear that they have always had a blindness in their hearts and minds. Consider 2 Corinthians 3:12–16.

> Therefore, since we have such hope, we use great boldness of speech-

Unlike Moses, who put a veil over his face so that the children of Israel could not look steadily at the end of what was passing away.

But their minds were blinded. For until this day the same veil remains unlifted in the reading of the Old Testament, because the veil is taken away in Christ.

But even to this day, when Moses is read, a veil lies on their heart.

Nevertheless when one turns to the Lord, the veil is taken away.

In Romans, Paul describes this blindness as being "in part ... until the fullness of the Gentiles has come in." His language in Romans indicates that there is a "godly remnant according to the election of grace" (Romans 11:5) who are coming to faith in Jesus Christ during the church age, but that the whole nation that survives the tribulation will be converted to faith in Jesus as their Messiah just before His glorious return.

10. **The Mystery of the Seven Stars (Revelation 1:20)**

The seven stars are defined for us in the passage as the "angels of the seven churches." The term *angels* literally means "sent ones, messengers," or in this case, the pastors of the seven churches of Asia Minor. The next two chapters in the Apocalypse consist of letters from Christ, the Head of the church, to the pastors of the seven churches located in an area which today is known as Turkey. The seven lampstands are also defined for us as the seven churches.

While the literal interpretation presents us with a prophetic look into the immediate future of these seven churches, it also allows for a challenging portrayal of seven divisions within the church age that has also unfolded precisely as foretold.

11. **The Mystery of Babylon the Harlot (Revelation 17:5, 7)**

History reveals that many of the false religious rituals and doctrines that came out of Babylon were incorporated into the church under Constantine the Great and the development of the Roman Catholic Church. Many commentators identify "Babylon the Harlot" as the Roman church, but this is likely too narrow a view of this passage.

It probably refers to the religious system controlled by the False Prophet during the reign of the Antichrist. Such a system is empowered by satanic delusion and pseudo supernaturalism that could deceive, "if possible, the very elect" (Matthew 24:24).

The Church of Rome provides a convenient platform for Satan to erect his one-world church system that will produce a host of Jewish and Christian martyrs during the tribulation. It would be so simple for the False Prophet to assume control of the Roman Church and massage its trappings for his own doctrinal and religious purposes.

Of one thing we are very sure. Religion is one of the devil's most successful and powerful tools for keeping lost sinners in the dark and estranged from the truth as it is only found in Jesus Christ.

12. The Mystery of God (Revelation 10:7; 11:15–19)

The Old Testament has much to say about God. His divine attributes are set forth in precept and historic illustration. The message of the Mosaic Covenant was that Yahweh was the one and only God. Monotheism was the testimony of the Lord's witnesses in a polytheistic world. In Israel, one of the most important passages of the scriptures was referred to as the Shema, found in Deuteronomy 6:4–5, which declares,

Hear, O Israel: The LORD our God, the LORD is one!

You shall love the LORD your God with all your heart, with all your soul, and with all your strength.

The mystery of God is that His Godhead consists of three divine Persons: Father, Son, and Holy Spirit. Plurality within God was suggested in many places, including the creation account in Genesis 1:26. "Then God said, 'Let us make man in Our image, according to Our likeness …'"

The New Testament revelation provided us with the elements of this doctrine that were not clarified to Israel in the Old Testament. There is only one God in His Essence, but He exists in three Persons. A rule of thumb for understanding the doctrine of the Trinity is this: "Never divide the Essence of God or confuse the Persons of God."

If you divide the Essence of God, you become a Tritheist. If you confuse the Persons of God, you become a Modalist or a Unitarian.

God exists as Father, Son, and Holy Spirit. Each Person in the Godhead possesses all of the divine attributes of the

Essence of God coequally and independently with the other two Persons of the Trinity. The Father is God, the Son is God, and the Spirit is God, but the Father is not the Son, the Son is not the Spirit, and the Spirit is not the Father.

Notice Romans 1:20.

> For since the creation of the world His invisible attributes are clearly seen, being understood by the things that are made, even His eternal power and Godhead, so that they are without excuse ...

The universe was created to reflect the Trinity of the Godhead! It consists of space, matter, and time. Space possesses all the characteristics of the universe. Matter possesses all the characteristics of the universe. Time possesses all the characteristics of the universe. But it is obvious that source is not matter, and that matter is not time, and that time is not space.

In fact, space is also a triunity consisting of length, width, and height. Length possesses all of the characteristics of space, as do width and height. Yet clearly length is not width, width is not height, and height is not length!

So is matter a triunity! It consists of energy, motion, and phenomena. Energy possesses all the characteristics of matter. Motion possesses all of the characteristics of matter. Phenomena possess all the characteristics of matter. Yet clearly energy is not motion, motion is not phenomena, and phenomena is not energy.

Well, as you would expect, time is a triunity made up of future, present, and past. Time does not flow from the past through the present into the future but just the opposite. The future possesses all the characteristics of time, the present possesses all the characteristics of time, and the past possesses all the characteristics of time. Yet obviously the future is not the present, the present is not the past, and the past is not the future.

In each case cited above, the universe itself, including each of its triunity components of space, matter, and time, reflects precisely the relationships described in scripture about the Father, Son, and Holy Spirit in the Trinity that created them all!

The focus of this book will be based on the fifth mystery listed above: the mystery of the indwelling Christ. This is a subject that should warm the hearts of all believers because the key to everything that we need to live the Christian life is provided through the unravelling of this New Testament mystery!

THE MASTER'S TOUCH

During my pastorate in Toronto, we celebrated the centennial anniversary of the congregation. Invitations to our weekend of special events were mailed all over Canada and the USA to those who attended our Sunday school during the 1940s, 1950s, and 1960s.

One couple drove all the way up to Toronto from Florida where they were living as retirees. Their marriage had fallen on hard times, largely because of his alcoholism. Normally he was a gentleman and very kind to his wife and family, but when he was drunk, he became angry and abusive. They had discussed bringing their marriage to an end, but they hoped that their trip to Toronto might give them a new lease on life.

During Saturday afternoon, crowds of people enjoyed displays of pictures and collections of items and awards that had been kept in the archives of the church. Also, a series of ancient pictures had been produced in a slideshow that caused a lot of laughter and conversations.

We had a great banquet that evening and transferred from the fellowship room in the basement to the auditorium upstairs for an evening service. Hymns and special music prepared the way for a message from God's Word. The theme of the message was the contrast between the book of church membership and the Lamb's Book of Life! Your name may be found in the church's membership book, but you could still be disqualified for admission to heaven! Only those who have received Jesus as Savior and Lord will be granted entry into the heavenly home of the Father, Son, and Holy Spirit.

Following the Saturday evening service, the couple returned to the apartment where they were staying and had a terrible argument. He was determined to go out to a local bar and find some old friends who would join him in getting drunk. His wife stood in his way as he headed toward the apartment door. He shouted at her to get out of his way, and she replied, "You really want what the pastor was talking about tonight! You want to find peace with God, yourself, and all of us! Isn't that the truth?" He stood there with tears in his eyes, and his chin was quivering.

She led him to the couch where they both knelt down and prayed to the Lord for forgiveness and invited Jesus to take over their lives. In that brief moment of time, the Master's touch set him free from his bondage to alcoholism, and their marriage was renewed to a partnership of love in Christ!

In the years to follow, this dedicated couple won many souls to Christ and ministered to couples that were struggling with their marriages. Oh, what a difference our Savior makes when He becomes your Lord!

Chapter Two

THE MYSTERY OF THE AGES

To grasp the immense significance of this concept of our faith, we need to compare the impact of two different days of Pentecost. Both of these celebrate the birthday of a major administration or dispensation of God.

The first Day of Pentecost is described in the Old Testament book of Exodus. One man was with God in the upper regions, where he received the divine revelation of the Law. Upon his descent from that remarkable place, he confronted the debauchery and depravity of the chosen people. According to Archbishop Ussher's chronology, Moses received the Ten Commandments on Mount Sinai in the year 1445 BC.

When Moses descended from Mount Sinai carrying the two stone tables of the Law, he discovered that the children of Israel, with the complicity of his brother Aaron, the high priest, had fallen into deep moral and spiritual sin. They had made a golden calf out of their gold and collections of jewelry provided by the ladies, and they were worshipping the idol amid sexual and moral sin.

The holy wrath and righteous indignation of the Lord consumed Moses when he saw this disgraceful rebellion of God's chosen people. He threw down the tablets of stone.

The wrath and judgment of God were meted out against these corrupt and rebellious people. Exodus 32 describes how the sons of Levi obeyed the Lord's command to put their swords on their side and go in and out among the people from entrance to entrance of the camp killing brothers, companions, and neighbors. On that Day of Pentecost, Israel was born as a nation, God gave them His holy Law, they demonstrated their rebellion against Him, and three thousand unbelieving Jewish men were killed.

Old Testament believers were a part of a national covenant with Yahweh that was structured around the rite of circumcision and the rituals of ceremonial law. They were responsible to obey the 613 commandments contained in the Old Testament scriptures. These were subdivided into two main groups: the 248 mandatory laws (further subdivided into eighteen sections) and the 365 prohibition laws (further subdivided into thirteen sections). The Jews believed that there were 248 limbs in the human body, and 365 solar days in a year, so they found these numbers extremely helpful in the process of memorizing all 613 laws!

If you were born as a Gentile but desired fellowship with the One True God, you were forced to become a Jewish proselyte, submit to circumcision, and pursue a life of learning and obeying these laws of God. Some of the laws were viewed as moral law, which was a transcript of divine holiness; others were understood as ceremonial laws that controlled the sacrificial system in the tabernacle and then, later, the temple. A third group of laws applied to the civil and social lives of the Jewish community, dealing with the issues of property, finances, and even slavery.

This Mosaic Covenant contained both blessings and curses: blessings to those who obeyed God's laws and curses to those who rebelled against His commandments (see Deuteronomy 11:26–28). To make this distinction clear and memorable, God established an enormous object lesson.

As they were brought into the land of promise, they were instructed to designate Mount Gerizim as the mountain of blessing and Mount Ebal as the mountain of the curse. As the children of Israel passed between these mountains, they were required to recite the passage from Deuteronomy referred to above.

These two mountains were both about three thousand feet high, with Mount Ebal being about 230 feet higher than Mount Gerizim. They were close together and appropriate for this usage because of the centrality within Israel.

In spite of the many benefits and privileges that were enjoyed by the children of Israel in this covenant relationship with Yahweh, they wrote a sordid history of disobedience, spiritual adultery, and pagan idolatry that ultimately led them into the Babylonian captivity under Nebuchadnezzar. Only after seventy years under the yoke of bondage in Babylon were the people of Israel delivered from the sin of idolatry. The most amazing part of their historic record is that the Lord refrained from destroying them or casting them off from His presence forever!

The message of Jeremiah to Judah was precisely along these lines. In the book of Lamentations, he declared,

> Through the LORD's mercies we are not consumed, because His compassions fail not.
>
> They are new every morning; great is Your faithfulness. (Lamentations 3:22–23)

God had chosen Israel to be His witnesses in a pagan and polytheistic world. They were to stand up to the idolatry of the nations and declare that there is only one true God, and His name is Yahweh. Isaiah declared,

> "You are My witnesses," says the Lord, "And My servant whom I have chosen, that you may know and believe in Me, and understand that I am He. Before Me there was no god formed, nor shall there be after Me.
>
> I, even I am the LORD, and beside Me there is no Savior." (Isaiah 43:10–11)

The most serious issue facing an Old Testament believer was the presence of God. As Moses contemplated the instructions of the Lord to leave Mount Sinai and guide His chosen people to their Promised Land, he was filled with apprehension and doubt. He met with the Lord and pled for the clear evidence of God's presence. He said,

> "Now, therefore, I pray, if I have found grace in Your sight, show me now Your way, that I may know You and that I may find grace in Your sight. And consider that this nation is Your people."
>
> And He said, "My Presence shall go with you, and I will give you rest."
>
> Then he said to Him, "If Your Presence does not go with us, do not bring us up from here." (Exodus 33:13–15)

With the exception of Moses and Joshua, no other Old Testament believer could claim the promise "I will never leave you or forsake you." Everyone else faced the reality that God could withdraw His presence from them at any time!

Even David, a man "after God's own heart" (1 Samuel 13:14; 16:1–12; Psalm 89:20; Acts 13:22), lived in dread of the real possibility that God's Holy Spirit would withdraw from him. He had committed a host of sins, beginning with lust, adultery, deception, murder, a significant cover-up, hypocrisy, and the abuse of power in his position as king.

The Lord sent a prophet named Nathan to him to expose his guilt and transgressions to his own conscience and heart. In 2 Samuel 12:1–12, we find Nathan's parable about a rich man who owned flocks and herds but stole a poor man's one and only little ewe lamb. David was irate and demanded that the rich man be brought to justice, even declaring that the rich man would be required to repay fourfold to the poor man for his gross abuse of power and authority.

Nathan courageously declared to David that David himself was the offender in his story, that he had stolen Uriah's wife, and that he then arranged to have him killed in battle. David was crushed by his guilt and shame and deeply repented of his sin. He wrote two psalms dealing with this repentance (Psalm 32 and Psalm 51) and exalting the name of the Lord for His holiness and righteous judgment.

In the eleventh verse of Psalm 51, David prays that no New Testament Christian need ever utter. He writes, "Do not cast me away from Your presence, and do not take Your Holy Spirit from me."

Fast-forward to the Day of Pentecost described in Acts 2. On that day, 120 disciples of Jesus were waiting in the upper room. They were behind closed and locked doors for fear of the Jews. Suddenly they were baptized by the Holy Spirit into the body of Christ and the church was born. Instead of the Law of God, they received the Spirit of God and moved out with the message of the Gospel in holy boldness. Through the supernatural ministry of the newly born church, multitudes heard the message of the cross and the empty tomb in their own dialects. The result of this confrontation was that three thousand unbelieving Jewish men were brought into light out of darkness, into freedom out of bondage, and into life out of spiritual death!

Post-Pentecost believers are indwelt by the Holy Spirit in a permanent relationship that will never be revoked by God, no matter how badly we may behave! Jesus Himself was the One who made this promise clear. He said, "And I will pray the Father, and He will give you another Helper, that He may abide with you forever ... I will not leave you orphans; I will come to you"; "At that day you will know that I am in the Father, and you in Me, and I in you" (John 14:16, 18–19).

It is this startling truth that we want to examine and appropriate during the pages of this book. The concept is amazing and all-encompassing and precisely explains the secret of victory over the world, the flesh, and the devil and is the key that opens the door of powerful and effective Christian service. There are several serious implications that emerge from this concept of an indwelling Christ. Each of them is controversial and must be understood in the context of the gospel of Jesus Christ. It is this very Gospel that causes the church of Jesus Christ to be the object of hatred and persecution worldwide today.

The first implication is that all religions lead their followers to a lost eternity in hell!

Why does the world hate Christianity so intensely? The hatred springs up because of Christianity's message, which is considered bigoted, narrow-minded, and uncompromising. It was Jesus Christ Himself who said, "I am the way, the truth and the life. No one comes to the Father except through Me" (John 14:6).

It has been estimated conservatively that over 200 million believers in Jesus Christ wake up each day in a world that threatens their very existence. The twentieth century has been dubbed "the age of martyrdom" because more Christians died for their faith in those one hundred years than in all 1,900 years combined prior to that century. About 28 million Christians became martyrs in the century just completed. And 176,000 Christians are killed annually simply because of their faith in Christ!

The second implication rejects Judaism and its ritualism as false teaching. Only "a godly remnant according to the election of grace" (Romans 11:5) were able to see past the Mosaic Covenant and grasp the message of redemption by grace through faith plus nothing! These Jews were anticipating the coming of their Messiah in whom they placed their trust.

Paul's strong argument in the Epistle to the Galatians demonstrated that the Law was never given to Israel by Yahweh as a means of salvation but to clearly establish their guilt and sin before God, thus leading them to Christ (Galatians 2:16; 3:1–14, 19–25).

Jews cannot find acceptance with God simply because of their lineage or legalism. The plan of redemption has consistently been the same in both the Old Testament and New Testament. Salvation is a free gift provided by the grace of God through the sacrifice of His precious Son as an innocent substitute for those who put their trust in Him alone.

In Ephesians 2, Paul explains that both Jews and Gentiles are lost and in need of regeneration. He describes it as becoming a part of "one new man" that is called "the Body of Christ," the church (Ephesians 2:14–23). Gentiles no longer need to become proselytes to Judaism as was the case during the dispensation of law but are accepted on an equal footing with born-again Jews.

Thirdly, Christianity has departed from the true message of the Gospel over many centuries and has become a religion itself. As such, it is used by Satan to lead men and women to eternal destruction by replacing grace with works and Christ with church.

The Edict of Toleration in AD 315 by Emperor Constantine created a monster now known as the Roman Catholic Church. The merging of Christianity with Babylonian paganism has so distorted the truth of the Gospel that its message can barely be discerned in Roman doctrine. The authority of scripture has been replaced with the authority of the church, its councils, and its popes. The use of the confessional booth, the sale of indulgences, the Inquisition, the doctrine of purgatory, and the worship of the Virgin Mary and her "immaculate conception" (meaning that Mary was conceived without original sin) are doctrines and practices in the Roman church that are false and satanic in their origin.

Protestantism, unfortunately, only accomplished a partial reformation. Many denominations that identify themselves as "Protestant" have created their own brand of works, rituals, and traditions that blind their members to the simple truth of the Gospel of Jesus Christ!

The apostle Paul made this abundantly clear in his letter to Titus when he wrote,

> But when the kindness and love of God our Savior toward man appeared, not by works of righteousness which we have done, but according to His mercy He saved us, through the washing of regeneration and renewing of the Holy Spirit, whom He poured out on us abundantly through Jesus Christ our Savior, that having been justified by His grace we should become heirs according to the hope of eternal life. (Titus 3:4–7)

"The Mystery of the Ages"

Mystery 1: "Christ *in* You!"

Colossians 1:24–27

> I now rejoice in my sufferings for you, and fill up in
> my flesh what is lacking in the afflictions of Christ,
> for the sake of His Body, which is the Church,
>
> Of which I became a minister according to the
> stewardship from God which was given to me for
> you, to fulfill the Word of God,
>
> The mystery which has been hidden from ages and
> from generations, but now has been revealed to His
> saints,
>
> To them God has willed to make known what are
> the riches of the glory of this mystery among the
> Gentiles: which is Christ in you, the hope of glory.

When we were little children attending Sunday school, our teachers
used to tell us that we needed to ask Jesus to come into our hearts.
Skeptics have laughed about this concept, declaring that the concept
is absurd and dishonest. We were being misled into an emotional
religious experience that had no validity in logic or scripture.

Well, the skeptics were wrong!

It is not only logical and scriptural, but it is essential that Jesus Christ
be invited to take up personal and permanent residence within our
innermost being—our hearts!

The Day of Pentecost described in Acts 2:1–4 changed the whole idea of the presence of God in the lives of believers forever. Earlier in this chapter, we described the birthday of Israel on the Day of Pentecost when God gave Moses the Law and created a nation that would represent Him in a polytheistic world. The most essential core value of that revelation was that there is only one God in our universe and that all others are pretenders created in the heart of the father of lies!

Israel was established to be a witness for Yahweh to a pagan world, and they were required to maintain a life of separation from idols and the gods of the heathen people living around them. Israel was provided with the Law to control their lifestyle and communicate with them from their living God.

God's Holy Spirit was external to the Old Testament believers and would come upon them to provide supernatural power (as in the case of Samson, Judges 13:24–25) and wisdom (seen in the life of Solomon, 1 Kings 3:5–9).

This very nature of the ministry of the Holy Spirit was a heavy burden on the hearts of the Old Testament leaders because they could easily find that the Holy Spirit had withdrawn from them and their skills, strength or wisdom had vanished. Furthermore, they could never be absolutely sure of their eternal destiny. Many of them only expected to be "gathered to their fathers" in a "place of shades" called Sheol.

An ancient Gentile believer had a greater insight into eternity than these Israelite leaders when he said,

> For I know that my Redeemer lives, and He shall
> stand at last on the earth;

And after my skin is destroyed, this I know, that in my flesh I shall see God. (Job 19:25–26)

Only two Old Testament leaders received the promise from God that He would never leave them or forsake them. The first was Moses who then passed on the promise to Joshua (Deuteronomy 31:6–8; Joshua 1:5). This same promise is found in Hebrews 13:5, where every member of the body of Christ, the church, has been given this wonderful assurance!

On the Day of Pentecost in Acts 2, everything changed!

Mystery 2: Spiritual Unity

Ephesians 2:11–18

> Therefore remember that you, once Gentiles in the flesh—who are called "Uncircumcision" by what is called "Circumcision" made in the flesh by hands
>
> That at that time you were without Christ, being aliens from the commonwealth of Israel and strangers from the covenants of promise, having no hope and without God in the world.
>
> But now in Christ Jesus you who once were far off have been brought near by the blood of Christ.
>
> For He Himself is our peace, who has made both one, and has broken down the middle wall of separation,
>
> Having abolished in His flesh the enmity, that is, the law of commandments contained in ordinances,

so as to create one new man from the two, thus making peace,

And that He might reconcile both to God in one body through the cross, thereby putting to death the enmity.

And He came and preached peace to you who were afar off and to those who were near.

For through Him we both have access by one Spirit to the Father.

Ephesians 3:1–7

For this reason I, Paul, the prisoner of Christ Jesus for you Gentiles—If indeed you have heard of the dispensation of the grace of God which was given to me for you,

How that by revelation He made known to me the mystery (as I have briefly written already,

By which, when you read, you may understand my knowledge in the mystery of Christ),

Which in other ages was not made known to the sons of men, as it has been revealed by the Spirit to His holy apostles and prophets;

That the Gentiles should be fellow heirs, of the same body, and partakers in Christ through the gospel,

Of which I became a minister according to the gift of the grace of God given to me by the effective work of His power.

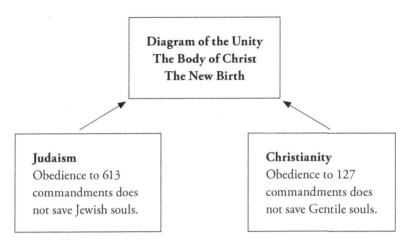

Both Jewish and Gentile people must be born again by faith in Christ alone for salvation! (See Ephesians 2:8–10; John 3:16; Acts 4:12; Romans 5:1; 8:1; 10:9–13; Galatians 2:16.)

The Holy Spirit took up personal residence within the bodies of the believers in Jesus. In this manner, He would abide with them and in them forevermore. The indwelling of the Holy Spirit in the body of a believer is the most significant change between the Old Testament and New Testament ministries of the Spirit of God.

New Testament believers are led and directed by the promptings of the Holy Spirit. He often urges us to take specific action that results in blessing and power. Divine appointments are produced by the leading of the Holy Spirit setting up conversations with those who are seeking the truth and those who are evangelists.

The Spirit calls individuals to surrender their lives, talents, time, and resources in full-time Christian service. Every believer is called to be a "full-time Christian," but some are set apart for the work of the ministry at home or abroad. Personally, that call came to me in a church service when I was a struggling thirteen-year-old suffering with an inferiority complex, convinced that I was not able to be successful academically, afraid to speak in crowds, and awkward in one-on-one conversations! I literally had nothing to offer the Lord for His kingdom work, but the Sovereign Lord who calls us also equips us and provides the grace to answer the call!

THE MASTER'S TOUCH

During one of my pastorates, we experienced a large harvest of souls into faith in Jesus Christ! The attendance in the church grew from eighty to 350. The highest attendance in our Sunday school reached 552 for our Christmas presentation.

Whenever a church experiences such growth, you can count on a satanic attack to distract from the ministry of the Holy Spirit. In the case of this church, we came into contact with a family whose mother was an active and legitimate witch! She practiced séances, trances, hypnotism, curses, and foretelling the future.

This lady had been involved in deep conversations with one of our strong lady believers. She became very convicted of her own sinfulness and of the darkness of the satanic influence in her heart and life over the years. We shared the Gospel with her one evening, and at the end of the presentation, this witch prayed to receive Jesus as her Savior and Lord. She renounced all the rituals and contacts she had with demonic spirits and claimed her freedom from this bondage through the blood of the Lamb and the power of His Spirit.

Several Sundays later, Mavis was baptized in our morning service and applied for membership along with her family as well. However, when Ann and I returned home, the phone was ringing in our kitchen, and a very upset lady was on the other end describing the mess they found in their house when they entered.

Poltergeist had taken place during her baptism! A large bag of potatoes stored in a cold room at the back entrance was opened and the potatoes now rotten were plastered all over the walls on the first floor. The potatoes were even found on the ceilings, dripping down from their rotten messes!

A team of deacons and me met with the family and we tackled two very important tasks. First, we cleaned every wall and ceiling that was filthy with the horrendous mess! Second, we walked with the family from room to room and pausing for prayer from the members of the team. At the end of this prayer walk, we brought the family together in the living room and gathered them with our hands on their backs and heads as we pled the blood of the Lord as their protection against Satan and his fallen angels!

From that point on, there were no future demonic activities in that house now dedicated to Bible studies, fellowship, and prayer meetings! Praise the Lord!

Chapter Three

A NEW COMMUNICATION

Many years ago, I was a student in seminary sitting under the teaching of Dr. George B. Fletcher in a series of lectures on the attributes of God. Dr. Fletcher was one of those men of God who impacted your life by his life as well as his academic skill! When he entered a room, you would sense the presence of the Lord in him.

As the final lecture concluded, Dr. Fletcher said, "Are there any questions?"

To my dismay, I discovered that my hand was raised, and my name was called out by Dr. Fletcher. "Yes, John. What is your question?"

The question I asked seemed impudent and rude!

I said, "Sir, so what?"

The beloved professor looked at me for a long time. Finally, he said, "I have known John since he was a little boy growing up in a godly home. I therefore assume that this question is not disrespectful or flippant! Next week I'll dedicate the entire class to an answer for John! Class dismissed."

The next week, my hand cramped up from writing so many copious notes recording Dr. Fletcher's powerful response to my question!

He began with the following comment:

> The question "So what?" is one of the most important questions you could ever ask when studying the Bible! "So what?" actually means: What is the application of the truth we have studied together? How does the doctrine of the attributes of God impact my values system? How does the character of God shape the decisions of my life? How does theology become a revelation to the depths of my soul?

That class session went by like lightning! Before we could grasp the deep significance of what we heard that day, the class was dismissed again!

The notes that I had taken that day traveled with me through the decades of ministry throughout Ontario and around the world! One day it was as if someone had turned on the light switch in my heart and mind! It came out of a heavy textbook written by Dr. Augustus H. Strong titled *Systematic Theology*.

He had classified the attributes of God under two categories.

1. THE ABSOLUTE OR IMMANENT ATTRIBUTES

There were the following three subsections under this heading:

1. Spirituality, Involving Life and Personality
2. Infinity, Seen in Self-Existence, Immutability, and Unity
3. Perfection, Consisting of Truth Love, and Holiness

These divine attributes belong to God alone and will never be shared by Him with any of His creatures. If they could be found in the creatures, they would claim to be the Creator!

That was what took place one day on the shore of the Pacific Ocean. Shirley MacLean had engaged in a conversation with John Heard in a movie called *Out on a Limb*. Shirley stood in the waters of the Pacific, and urged on by John Heard, she chanted over and over again, "I am God! I am God! I am God!"

How disappointing it must have been to Shirley to exit from the Pacific waters and discover that she was just the same as when she entered them! She was not God! Some day she will stand in His presence and give an account of everything that she has done in the body, whether good or bad!

2. THE RELATIVE OR TRANSITIVE ATTRIBUTES

Unlike the absolute or immanent attributes of God, the relative or transitive attributes are "a New Communication" from God, even though they have existed from eternity past! They are new to us by the unfolding of the inspired biblical record in the age of grace or of the church of Christ.

Once again, there are three groupings of these divine attributes.

    A. Attributes Related to Space, Matter, and Time
        i. Eternity
       ii. Immensity

    B. Attributes Related to Creation
        i. Omnipresence
       ii. Omniscience

    iii. Omnipotence

  C. Attributes Related to Moral Beings
     i. Transitive Truth
       (Veracity and Faithfulness)
     ii. Transitive Love
       (Mercy and Goodness)
    iii. Transitive Holiness
       (Justice and Righteousness)

These last attributes are extremely significant to the human race because we are the only creatures that can receive and grow in any of the divine attributes! This is what Peter was referring to in his Second Epistle (2 Peter 1:2–4; emphasis mine).

> Grace and peace be multiplied to you in the knowledge of God and Jesus Christ our Lord,
>
> As His divine power has given to us all things that pertain to life and godliness, through the knowledge of Him who called us by glory and virtue,
>
> By which have been given to us exceedingly great and precious promises, <u>that through these you may be partakers of the divine nature</u>, having escaped the corruption that is in the world through lust.

The only way that a human being could be a partaker of the divine nature is through the mystery of the indwelling Christ!

Consider these well-known scriptures:

John 14:15–20

> If you love me, keep My commandments.

And I will pray the Father, and He will give you another (of the same kind) Helper (Paraclete), that He may abide with you forever—

The Spirit of truth, whom the world cannot receive, because it neither sees Him nor knows Him; but you know Him, for He dwells with you, and will be IN YOU.

A little while longer and the world will see Me no more, but you will see Me. Because I live, you will live also.

At that day you will know that I am in My Father, and you in Me, and I in you.

In his epistles to the Corinthian church, Paul brought up this same miraculous and mysterious concept!

1 Corinthians 6:19, 20

Or do you not know that your body is the temple (naos) of the Holy Spirit Who is IN YOU, Whom you have from God, and you are not your own?

For you were bought with a price; therefore glorify God in your body and in your spirit, which are God's.

2 Corinthians 6:14–18

Do not be unequally yoked together with unbelievers. For what fellowship has righteousness with lawlessness? And what communion has light with darkness?

And what accord has Christ with Belial? Or what part has a believer with an unbeliever?

And what agreement has the temple [naos] of God with idols? For you are the temple of the Living God. As God has said,

"I will dwell in them and walk among them. I will be their God, and they shall be My people."

Therefore

"Come out from among them and be separate, says the Lord. Do not touch what is unclean, and I will receive you."

"I will be a Father to you, and you shall be My sons and daughters, says the LORD Almighty."

I deliberately inserted in brackets the Greek word *naos*. Why? Because there are two words in Greek that could be translated into the English as "temple."

The first word is *hieron*, which includes everything about the temple, including the temple mount on which it was built. It includes the seven steps up to the great or outer court, then the eight steps and the upper or inner court, which contained the large bronze altar where the priests offered the sacrifices to Yahweh.

The Holy of Holies, naos, was only available on one day of the year, the day of Yom Kippur. It could only be entered by the high priest following the rigid regulations preparing him for surviving the presence of the infinitely holy God.

The high priest wore holy garments with little bells attached to the bottom hem. As the high priest moved about in the naos, the other priests behind the veil could hear the little bells tinkling. That was wonderful to them because the high priest was still alive, the offerings and incense had been accepted by the Lord, and the atonement of Israel had been accomplished for another year!

There was only one piece of furniture in the Holy of Holies. It was the Ark of the Covenant, made of acacia wood and plated inside and out with pure gold. The lid on the Ark of the Covenant was called "the mercy seat" with two golden cherubim facing toward each other on the top. Between the cherubim was the Shekinah glory of God, a cloud in which Yahweh appeared above the mercy seat.

The word for "mercy seat" in the New Testament occurs in Romans 3:25. "Whom God set forth as a propitiation *(hilasterios)* by His blood through faith ..."

The message for us today is that Jesus Christ is our mercy seat! He is the presence of the Living God, abiding in our hearts by faith! The presence of the Living God abides within our hearts and is only a prayer away!

The third grouping of these attributes of God is extremely important to us today. Why? Because the relevance of these three categories is demonstrated to our world when the Lord transforms a sinner into a saint in a split second of time! Our sanctification is an act at conversion and a process throughout Christian life and service.

The three attributes of God found here are necessary for our spiritual maturity and godliness in our behavior. They also enable us to be productive in our service to the Lord Jesus as we use our talents and spiritual gifts for His glory. These three attributes are part of the "communicable attributes" of God. They can be "communicated" to redeemed saints who are indwelt by the Holy Spirit!

Paul made it perfectly clear that unsaved people cannot enjoy these blessings.

1 Corinthians 2:14

> But the natural man does not receive the things of the Spirit of God, for they are foolishness to him; nor can he know them, because they are spiritually discerned.

Just ahead of this verse is another passage that is usually quoted out of context.

1 Corinthians 2:9

> But it is written: "Eye has not seen, nor ear heard, nor have entered into the heart of man the things which God has prepared for those who love Him."

Most people stop here and interpret the passage quoted from Isaiah 64:4 and 65:17, and they conclude that these things cannot be understood by man's finite mind! The context interprets the verse quite differently.

1 Corinthians 2:10

> But God has revealed them to us through His Spirit. For the Spirit searches all things, yes, the deep things of God.

The transitive truth of God contains two powerful attributes that He wants us to experience in our lives as well!

- The Veracity of God

God cannot do anything that contradicts His holiness; therefore, He says what He means and means what He says!

Hebrews 6:17–20

> Thus God, determining to show more abundantly to the heirs of promise the immutability of His counsel, confirmed by an oath, that by two immutable things, in which it is impossible for God to lie, we might have strong consolation, who have fled for refuge to lay hold of the hope set before us.
>
> This hope we have as an anchor of the soul, both sure and steadfast, and which enters the Presence behind the veil, where the Forerunner has entered for us, even Jesus, having become High Priest forever according to the order of Melchizedek.

John 14:1–6

> Let not your hearts be troubled; you believe in God, believe also in Me.
>
> In My Father's house are many mansions. If it were not so, I would have told you! I go to prepare a place for you.
>
> And if I go and prepare a place for you, I will come again and receive you to Myself; that where I am, there you may be also.
>
> And where I go you know, and the way you know.

Thomas said to Him, "Lord, we do not know where you are going, and how can we know the way?"

Jesus said to him, "I am the Way, the Truth and the Life.' No one comes to the Father except through Me."

The reality of a place called "heaven" is predicated on the veracity of Jesus Christ! He is Truth personified. The Lord of the Bible cannot lie, misrepresent the facts, or exaggerate the details! An integral part of His Being is integrity.

- The Faithfulness of God

God cannot make a promise that He won't keep! Nor does He look for a loophole that allows Him to escape from His own word.

Lamentations 3:22, 23

Through the Lord's mercies we are not consumed ...

God would be perfectly just and right if He were to destroy every human being on planet Earth! Why? Because He is infinitely holy, and we are totally depraved!

Habakkuk 1:13

You are of purer eyes than to behold evil, and cannot look on wickedness ...

Lamentations 2:22–23

Through the Lord's mercies we are not consumed because His compassions fail not.

They are new every morning; Great is Your faithfulness.

2 Corinthians 1:20

For all the promises of God in Him (Jesus) are "Yes", and "Amen", to the glory of God through us!

Deuteronomy 7:9

Therefore know that the LORD your God, He is God, the Faithful God, who keeps His covenant and mercy for a thousand generations with those who love Him and keep His commandments ...

Isaiah 49:7

Thus says the LORD, the Redeemer of Israel, their Holy One, to Him Whom man despises, to Him Whom the nation abhors, to the Servant of rulers: kings shall see and arise, princes also shall worship, because the LORD Who is faithful, the Holy One of Israel; and He has chosen you.

1 John 1:9

If we confess our sins, He is faithful and just to forgive us our sins and to cleanse us from all unrighteousness.

He is faithful because He promised to forgive us of all our sins!

He is just because He died on the cross and rose again from the tomb; therefore, He paid the penalty for all of our sins and purchased a place in heaven for us that He offers as a free gift.

As Jesus was being crucified on the cross, He cried out seven expressions. One was a single Greek word: *tetelesthai.*

Our English versions translate this word to mean "It is finished!"

Jesus did complete the work for which He was born! He finished fulfilling the Law and the prophets as the Messiah. Yes!

Archaeologists found some documents in Alexandria, Egypt, that were contracts similar to our credit cards today. When the final payment was made on this financing plan, the lender printed in capital letters, diagonally across the document, "TETELESTHAI!"

In this case, the word means, "PAID IN FULL!"

Romans 8:28, 29

> And we know that all things work together for good
> to those who love God, to those who are called
> according to His purpose.
>
> For whom He foreknew, He also predestined to be
> conformed to the image of His Son, that He might
> be the first born among many brethren.

God's purpose is to transform sinners into saints in a miraculous and a mysterious way! Our conversion experiences are unique and a living example of the grace of God to our lost relatives, neighbors, friends, and even our enemies!

Philippians 1:27

> Only let your conduct be worthy of the gospel of
> Christ, so that whether I come and see you or am
> absent, I may hear of your affairs, that you stand

fast in one spirit, with one mind, striving together
for the faith of the gospel ...

1 Peter 2:9–10

> But you are a chosen generation, a royal priesthood,
> a holy nation, His own special people, that you may
> proclaim the praises of Him who called you out of
> darkness into His marvelous light;
>
> Who once were not a people but are now the people
> of God, who had not obtained mercy, but now have
> obtained mercy.

The acid test of Christianity is not theology but *transformation*.
Far too many people in our generation claim to have experienced
the new birth but have shown no radical change in their behavior,
in their values, in their priorities system, or in their goals, dreams,
and ambitions! Too many professing Christians are not possessing
Christians!

One of the most effective authors that I've had the privilege of
reading has been called a prophet to the preachers. His name is
Leonard Ravenhill, and his book *Why Revival Tarries* has stirred my
heart for many years.

In the foreword written by A. W. Tozer, I came across the following
paragraph:

> Toward Leonard Ravenhill it is impossible to be
> neutral. His acquaintances are divided pretty neatly
> into two classes, those who love and admire him
> out of all proportion and those who hate him with
> perfect hatred ... The reader will either close its

pages and seek a place of prayer or he will toss it away in anger, his heart closed to its warnings and appeals.

Leonard Ravenhill penned the following poem in *Why Revival Tarries:*

> Could a mariner sit idle if he heard the drowning cry?
> Could a doctor sit in comfort and just let his patient die?
> Could a fireman sit idle, let men burn and give no hand?
> Can you sit at ease in Zion with the world around you DAMNED?

The issue that stands before us at this point is how? How can we become a reasonable facsimile of Jesus Christ in this old world of sin and compromise?

The answer lies in an inward renewal through the impact of scripture on our minds. That's what Paul was addressing in Ephesians 4.

Ephesians 4:17–24

> This I say, therefore, and testify in the Lord, that you should no longer walk as the rest of the Gentiles walk, in the futility of their mind,
>
> Having their understanding darkened, being alienated from the life of God, because of the ignorance that is in them, because of the blindness of their heart;
>
> Who, being past feeling, have given themselves over to lewdness, to work all uncleanness with greediness.

But you have not so learned Christ,

If indeed you have heard Him and been taught by Him, as the truth is in Jesus;

That you put off concerning your former conduct, the old man which grows corrupt according to deceitful lusts,

And <u>be renewed in the spirit of your mind,</u>

<u>And that you put on the new man which was created according to God, in true righteousness and holiness.</u>

As we move along this line of reasoning, we'll be unpacking the divine plan for our growth in grace and the knowledge of Christ Jesus our Lord (2 Peter 3:18).

The challenge before us is to discover how God's plan for our sanctification will actually cause us to be "renewed in the spirit of our minds."

We will approach this stage of our study in the next chapter.

THE MASTER'S TOUCH

Martha was in her eighties when she came on a "Vision Tour" offered by HCJB Australia to reveal the development of our new radio station. Miraculously, the federal government of Australia reversed their long-held position that all shortwave radio licenses could only be held by the government.

The offer of four licenses was extended to HCJB with a short time limit for activating the broadcasts produced in our studios in Melbourne and then sent by land line over four thousand kilometers to a small town called Kununurra in the North-West Territories.

Martha was one of our first tourists who joined together in the city of Darwin to travel by a small bus over the outback to our transmitter site on a small farm on the outskirts of Kununurra. This was the town that was well known for its diamond mines and the retail outlets marketing the very beautiful diamond jewelry. She was standing at the display counter examining a ring worth AU $2,000 when she told the clerk that she wanted to take time to pray about it! He was stunned by this request but quickly recovered to encourage her to return the next day since he would hold it for her.

The next day Martha informed him that she had been convinced that her $2,000 could be used in a much better way! She was going to give it to her daughter and husband to cover their expenses for the Vision Tour the following year!

The next year the tour began in Darwin with a Sunday morning church service held in a local Baptist church. Seated at the back was Martha's daughter Brenda with her husband, Paul. A Gospel message was presented to the gathering that day with a challenge to pray a prayer of commitment to Jesus Christ as Savior and Lord. When I asked for hands of those who had prayed that prayer with me to be raised, the hands of Brenda and Paul were the first to respond!

A few days later, we were at our station in Kununurra and Brenda was able to phone her mother with the good news. I'll never forget what she said to start the conversation with Martha!

She said, "Mother, you have a brand-new diamond. No, you have two new diamonds! Paul and I have received Jesus as our Lord!" Martha was overwhelmed with joy and excitement. Her son-in-law came from a mixed family that had a number of aboriginal people in the family tree. Because of the abuse of alcohol and drugs, many of these people were in bondage to demonic spirits and addiction to substance abuse, resulting in mood swings and depression.

Paul was set free from this entire heritage in that moment in Darwin Baptist Church when Jesus transformed him into a new creation! Old things had passed away, and all things had become new!

Ann and I were privileged to stay in Paul and Brenda's home for a few days where we were able to lead their son to a saving knowledge of Jesus! We became good friends with this family and exchanged cards and letters from then on. (We returned home to Canada in the fall of 2006!)

Someday soon we will meet with Martha, Brenda, and Paul in our heavenly home where we will adore, worship, and serve our precious Lord who changes each of us with a simple touch of the Master's hand!

Chapter Four

A NEW CHRISTLIKENESS

The new Christlikeness is the expected change in the behavior and attitude of those who have been born again. Unfortunately, many professing Christians are caught up in the pressure of society and their worldly heroes.

It has been observed that there is so much of the world in today's churches that we cannot distinguish between the two! This is not the purpose of the Trinity in heaven for His people! We have been declared to be *salt* and *light* by the Lord Himself (Matthew 5:13–16).

1 John 2:15–17

> Do not love the world or the things of the world. If anyone loves the world, the love of the Father is not in him.
>
> For all that is in the world—the lust of the flesh, the lust of the eyes, and the pride of life—is not of the Father but is of the world.
>
> And the world is passing away, and the lust of it; but he who does the will of God abides forever.

1 Peter 2:11–12

> Beloved, I beg you as sojourners and pilgrims, abstain from fleshly lusts which war against the soul,
>
> Having your conduct honorable among the Gentiles, that when they speak against you as evildoers, they may, by your good works which they observe, glorify God in the day of visitation.

Romans 12:1–2

> I beseech you therefore, brethren, by the mercies of God, that you present your bodies as a living sacrifice, holy, acceptable to God, which is your reasonable (rational) service.
>
> And do not be conformed to this world, but be transformed by the renewing of your mind, that you may prove what is that good, and acceptable, and perfect will of God.

Romans 2:4

> Or do you despise the riches of His goodness, forbearance, and longsuffering, not knowing that the goodness of God leads you to repentance?

Repentance is the evidence of saving faith! These two elements are like the two sides on a coin. You can't have one without the other, but saving faith is demonstrated by repentance. Paul explains that an unsaved man is not able to make the 180-degree turnabout that we expect him to make!

1 Corinthians 2:14

> But the natural man does not receive the things of
> the Spirit of God, for they are foolishness to him;
> nor can he know them, because they are spiritually
> discerned.

Metanoia (repentance) means "change your mind; change the way
you think." If you change the way that you think, you will also
change the way you behave!

In chapter 4, we described the impact of being filled with the Holy
Spirit (Ephesians 5:18). The Greek word for being filled is *play-ro-o*,
and it has three basic meanings.

1. It describes the wind that fills the sail on a boat and propels
    the vessel over the water.
2. It is used to describe the function of salt sprinkled on the
    surface of a roast before it's placed in the oven. In this case,
    it permeates the roast and enhances its flavor as it cooks.
3. When play-ro-o is used to describe a relationship between
    two persons, it refers to one controlling the other.

Since the Holy Spirit is a Person of the Trinity, He will control us when
we allow Him to fill us. This usage of the word is in the present tense,
indicating continuous action; thus, we are to keep being filled with the
Holy Spirit. Second, the verb is used in the imperative mood, which
requires our obedience to God's commandment. Third, the verb is
used in the passive voice, declaring that being filled with the Holy
Spirit is something done to us not by us. We are required to surrender
to the Lordship of Christ through the ministry of the Holy Spirit.

The Spirit-filled believer is transformed by the direction and
enablement given by God's grace. Consider the following scriptures:

In his Second Epistle, Peter makes an amazing statement.

2 Peter 1:2–4

> Grace and peace be multiplied to you in the knowledge of God and of Jesus our Lord.
>
> As His divine power has given to us all things that pertain to life and godliness, through the knowledge of Him who called us by glory and virtue,
>
> By which have been given to us exceedingly great and precious promises, that through these you may be <u>partakers of the divine nature</u>, having escaped the corruption that is in the world through lust.

How is it possible for lost sinners to become partakers of the divine nature? It was called the new birth by Jesus when He spoke with Nicodemus (John 3:3–8).

Paul described this conversion as receiving a new nature. Unfortunately, we also have our old natures that are fallen and prone to disobedience and rebellion against the Lordship of Jesus Christ (Galatians 5:17).

The so-what question that I asked Dr. Fletcher many years ago is the foundation for this book, and especially for this section in it! How is it possible for us to "partake of the divine nature" as mentioned by Peter above?

How does God transfer some of His divine attributes to His redeemed children? The answer is found in part of the ministry of the Holy Spirit to born-again believers. What does He give us that will transform a lost sinner into a saint that thinks like, speaks like, acts like, and reacts like such a holy Creator God?

Much of the answer we are seeking is found in Galatians 5:19–23.

> Now the works of the flesh are evident, which are: adultery, fornication, uncleanness, lewdness,
>
> Idolatry, sorcery, hatred, contentions, jealousies, outbursts of wrath, selfish ambitions, dissensions, heresies,
>
> Envy, murders, drunkenness, revelries and the like; of which I tell you beforehand, just as I told you in time past, that those who practice such things will not inherit the kingdom of God.

Now consider the contrast.

> But the fruit of the Spirit is love, joy, peace, longsuffering, kindness, goodness, faithfulness, gentleness, self-control. Against such there is no law.

Observations

1. The noun "fruit" describes a singular subject.
2. The singular verb "is" reflects the singular subject. Paul is not writing about "fruits" but fruit.
3. This singular fruit of the Holy Spirit has nine characteristics or attributes.
4. Each of these attributes provides us with a picture of godly behavior.
5. The nine characteristics appear to represent three relationships in our new Christian experience.

The outcome of this study is absolutely astounding! Let's take a closer look.

1. THE UPWARD RELATIONSHIP

The upward relationship produces the first two divine attributes known as the *transitive truth:* God's *veracity* and His *faithfulness.* The purpose of God for us is that we, too, should stand out in our society as people who are honest and true in all relationships and that we should be noted for our faithfulness: we say what we mean, and we mean what we say!

This transitive truth is produced in our spirits and minds through the filling and fruit of the indwelling Holy Spirit. We'll examine the nine characteristics of the singular fruit of the Spirit in reference to the transitive attributes of God.

The first three characteristics of the *fruit of the Spirit* are "love, joy, peace."

These words describe our *upward relationship* with our triune God: Father, Son, and Holy Spirit.

2. THE OUTWARD RELATIONSHIP

The second set of three attributes of God in Galatians 5:22–23 is "longsuffering, kindness, and goodness."

The "Christlikeness" described in the fruit of the Spirit does not entail goals or targets for which we are struggling within our personal relationships with other people! Some people are far from loveable, and they frequently bring out our old natures!

The "fruit of the Spirit" is singular but described in this passage with nine characteristics! How is this possible?

The fruit of the Spirit is the Christlikeness that we are expected to demonstrate in a fallen world!

How?

Through the inward relationship.

3. The Inward Relationship

The final three words used by Paul in Galatians 5:22–23 are "faithfulness, gentleness, and self-control."

The secret of this passage is surrendering your will and ego to the Lordship of Jesus Christ continuously.

In Ephesians 5:18, Paul wrote, "And do not be drunk with wine, in which is dissipation; but be filled with the Spirit."

The word used in the Greek language is *play-ro-o,* which means "surrender to His control over your old nature!"

The verb is used here in the present tense and imperative mood. That means that you need to be filled with the Spirit continuously, and to ignore such a commandment is sinful disobedience!

When the Spirit of God is in control of your nature, He will produce the following:

A. The Love of God

Agape love has been demonstrated for us on Calvary's cross, where our sins were expunged from God's record, never to condemn us again (Romans 5:8; 1 John 3:16; 4:9–10).

The wonder of the Gospel of Christ is that God hates all sin but loves all sinners. John 3:16 is "the gospel in a nutshell."

> For God so loved the world that He gave His only
> begotten Son, that whoever believes in Him should
> not perish but have everlasting life.

Many Christians have prayed to receive God's wonderful gift of His love through Christ, but they still live in anxiety and fear that they may not be admitted into God's heavenly home! They have not discovered the difference between the feeling of guilt and the reality of guilt! The feeling of guilt may be the result of satanic accusations reminding you of the sins of the past.

When a Christian sins, they lose the joy of their salvation, but they don't lose the everlasting gift of God's love purchased by Jesus through His death, burial, and resurrection. Salvation becomes yours by grace through faith plus *nothing!*

Ephesians 2:8–10

> For by grace you have been saved through faith, and
> that not of yourselves; it is the gift of God,
>
> Not of works, lest anyone should boast.
>
> For we are His workmanship, created in Christ Jesus
> for good works, which God prepared beforehand
> that we should walk in them.

Frederick M. Lehman wrote a hymn made popular through the rich voice of George Beverly Shea at the Billy Graham crusades.

> The love of God is greater far than tongue or pen could ever tell,
> It goes beyond the highest star and reaches to the lowest hell;
> The guilty pair, bowed down with care God gave His Son to win:
> His erring child He reconciled and pardoned from his sin.
>
> Could we with ink the ocean fill and were the skies of parchment made,
> Were every stalk on earth a quill and every man a scribe by trade,
> To write the love of God above would drain the ocean dry,
> Nor could the scroll contain the whole tho' stretched from sky to sky.
>
> O love of God, how rich and pure!
> How measureless and strong!
> It shall forevermore endure—the saints' and angels' song!

B. The Joy of the Lord

The joy of the Lord shall be our strength (Nehemiah 8:10) and is ours forever through the indwelling Holy Spirit who witnesses with our spirits that we are the children of God (Romans 8:14–17). Jesus promised His followers that they will be filled with His joy (John 15:11; 16:20, 24).

The tragedy of church history is the unbelieving believers! Consider what the writer of the book of Hebrews said.

> Beware, brethren, lest there be in any of you an evil heart of unbelief in departing from the living God! (Hebrews 3:12)

Jeremiah saw the same sinful behavior among those in Israel, and he rebuked them for their departure from Yahweh.

> For My people have committed two evils: they have forsaken Me, the Fountain of Living Waters, and hewn for themselves cisterns—broken cisterns that can hold no water! (Jeremiah 2:13)

Isaiah echoed the same condemnation with these words:

> Therefore the LORD said: "Inasmuch as these people draw near with their mouths and honor Me with their lips, but have removed their hearts far from Me, and their fear toward Me is taught by the commandment of men …" (Isaiah 29:13)

None other but the Lord Jesus Himself made the same condemnation.

> Not everyone who says to Me "Lord, Lord," shall enter the kingdom of heaven, but he who does the will of My Father in heaven.

> Many will say to Me in that day, "Lord, Lord, have we not prophesied in Your Name, cast out demons in Your Name, and done many wonders in Your Name"?

And then I will declare to them, "I never knew you; depart from Me, you who practice lawlessness!" (Matthew 7:21–23)

When Jesus becomes your Savior, He also becomes the Lord of your life! How can you profess to be His redeemed child while you complain, criticize, curse, and swear when you think no one is listening? How can you profess to be born again when your outlook on life is one of anxiety and/or anger?

Confess the sin of unbelief that has overtaken your heart, and let His Spirit fill you with thanksgiving, adoration, and praise for who He is, and what He has done! (See Philippians 4:4–7; 1 Thessalonians 5:16–19; Hebrews 13:15, 16.)

C. The Peace of God

(Romans 5:1; John 14:1–4, 27; Philippians 4:6, 7, 9)

The amazing truth as we examine this concept is that God intends to share His transitive truth with us through the indwelling Holy Spirit.

Because we have received His love, joy, and peace, we can embrace His veracity and faithfulness as a testimony to family, friends, and neighbors. We are the only Bibles some people will ever read, and we are transformed into His image so that we can evangelize the lost!

The acid test of this divine plan is the integrity of the believer. There is no room in God's program for hypocrites who drive people away from the church!

The two characteristics of all the children of God are the same two elements of transitive truth: *veracity and faithfulness!*

Psalm 139:23, 24

> Search me, O God, and know my heart; try me and
> know my anxieties;
>
> And see if there is any wicked way in me, and lead
> me in the way everlasting.

Revival in the church of Jesus Christ springs forth from a genuine inward cleansing that allows the believer to experience close fellowship with the Father, Son, and the Holy Spirit.

1 John 1:1–4

> That which was from the beginning, which we have
> heard, which we have seen with our eyes, which we
> have looked upon, and our hands have handled,
> concerning the Word of Life—
>
> The life was manifested, and we have seen, and bear
> witness, and declare to you that eternal life which
> was with the Father and was manifested to us—
>
> That which we have seen and heard we declare to
> you, that you also may have fellowship with us; and
> truly our fellowship is with the Father and with His
> Son Jesus Christ.
>
> And these things we write to you that your joy may
> be full.

Authenticity is not a new concept proposed by the millennials! It is an integral requirement for those who profess to be born-again Christians! One of the major complaints against the church throughout the generations is the hypocrisy that destroys the credibility of pastors, evangelists, televangelists, and the members who fill the seats in our church buildings!

We desperately need a revival in our churches that produces a biblical lifestyle giving evidence of the transformation only possible through Jesus Christ our Lord!

The apostle John draws a powerful application to the first four verses in chapter 1 of his First Epistle. In essence he says that you cannot have one foot in the kingdom of God and the other in the kingdom of Satan!

1 John 1:5–10

> This is the message that we heard from Him and declare to you, that God is light and in Him is no darkness at all.
>
> If we say that we have fellowship with Him, and walk in darkness, we lie and do not practice the truth.
>
> But if we walk in the light as He is in the light, we have fellowship with one another, and the blood of Jesus Christ His Son cleanses (keeps on cleansing) us from all sin.
>
> If we say that we have no sin, we deceive ourselves, and the truth is not in us.

If we confess our sins, He is faithful (because of His veracity) and just (because of His faithfulness) to forgive us our sins and to cleanse us from all unrighteousness.

His faithfulness exists because He cannot tell a lie. He cannot make a promise to us that He will not keep!

His veracity demands that He keep His promises based on His sacrificial atonement purchased with His precious blood shed on the cross and verified by His resurrection from the tomb!

The three attributes of the fruit of the Spirit are the application of God's veracity and faithfulness. These two aspects of God's transitive truth produce a transformation through our personal relationship with God and realized in our daily walk with the infinitely Holy One!

When the believer understands the miracle of God's saving grace, he or she enters the deeper life with God through the filling of the Spirit. This does not mean that everything in the believer's life will be free from pain, suffering, and even physical death. Nor does it mean that you can "name it and claim it" because you have found the secret behind the miracles of Jesus!

Consider the amazing promise written by David in Psalm 37:4. "Delight yourself in the LORD, and He shall give you the desires of your heart."

The basis of this promise lies in the condition required! "Delight yourself in the LORD ..."

When you come to the place where your heart, soul, and spirit are filled with "love, joy, and peace" with the Lord, then your desires will be transformed into the desires of the Lord! When your desires are the same as the ones that He has for you, then your prayer life will make a quantum leap into divine approval and power!

In our next chapter, we'll move on to the next set of the attributes of the fruit of the Spirit. These are the gifts of "longsuffering, kindness, and goodness."

THE MASTER'S TOUCH

On a Friday afternoon, I was busy setting up chairs for a staff prayer/ praise meeting the next day. We were sharing the gospel at the Leamington District Agricultural Fair in the arena.

In five days, we had led 205 people to a profession of faith in Jesus Christ! Among those many souls were two prostitutes, a drug dealer, a criminal gang leader, an alcoholic, and a daredevil stunt driver.

One of our young men came into the room accompanied by the foreman of the Hell Drivers who would be performing on Saturday afternoon. "Natch" (his nickname) was all muscle and toughness poured into a tight T-shirt and blue jeans.

Our conversation was brief and to the point! I heard myself saying to him, "Natch, you're only half a man! You are strong and skilled in physical things, but you have no relationship with the Lord God to whom you must give an account when your life on earth is done! In fact, a Christian can do what you do and a lot better! Why? Because a child of the Lord has His presence with them every moment of every day!"

Then Natch said, "OK, Preacher! You're on!"

I said, "What do you mean by that?"

He said, "Two o'clock tomorrow afternoon, you will ride with me! Be in the infield no later than 1:45!"

That afternoon I rode with Natch and his boss as they drove their cars at seventy-five miles per hour over jumps in the middle of the dirt track and then did power circles, crisscrossing each other. They then set up for a second run over the jumps.

As we sat in his car, Natch said, "You've done this before, haven't you?"

I said, "I have not ever ridden in such a car before, and certainly not over jumps at seventy-five miles per hour!"

Natch replied, "Well, why weren't you scared?"

I said, "Because you were not the driver! Over forty of my people have been praying for us since yesterday afternoon! I knew that Jesus was in charge of you and of this car, so there was no reason to be afraid!"

This friendship went on for months before Natch surrendered his life to the Lord Jesus Christ and eventually became a "Heaven Driver" instead of a "Hell Driver"!

His drunkenness, fighting, cursing, gambling, and womanizing came to a stop, and the new man found it impossible to keep on the lifestyle associated with his role on the Hell Drivers stunt team!

He resigned and settled his life as a testimony of what Jesus can do with a lost soul through His gift of grace.

Chapter Five

THE NEW COMPASSION

The conviction behind this book is that Jesus is the same "yesterday, today and forever" (Hebrews 13:8)!

He is the same Jesus who gave sight to the blind, healing to the lepers, the ability of speaking to the mute, and hearing for the deaf!

He alone is the One who spoke to the stormy sea and commanded the elements to be calm and peaceful!

The Jesus described in the New Testament is the God of creation, Providence, and grace, and He longs to have a close fellowship with us, in spite of our sinfulness and strong tendency to wander away from Him!

We have examined the *transitive truth,* which includes the two divine attributes of *veracity* and *faithfulness.* The purpose of our salvation is not to escape the flames of hell but to become just like the character of our Heavenly Father! We are destined by His grace to be just like Jesus.

We are chosen by God's grace in order that we might be effective ambassadors for Christ in a lost and rebellious world. We are transformed by the indwelling Holy Spirit and enabled to share the good news of eternal life.

> Therefore, if anyone is in Christ he is a new creation; old things have passed away; behold, all things have become new.
>
> Now all things are of God, who has reconciled us to Himself through Jesus Christ, and has <u>given to us the ministry of reconciliation.</u>
>
> That is that God was in Christ reconciling the world to Himself, not imputing their trespasses to them, and has committed to us the word of reconciliation.
>
> Now then, we are ambassadors for Christ, as though God were pleading through us; we implore you on Christ's behalf, be reconciled to God.
>
> For He has made Him Who knew no sin to be sin for us, that we might become the righteousness of God through Him. (2 Corinthians 5:17–21)

The apostle Paul begged the believers in the church at Rome that they would take seriously this concept of representing the Father, Son, and Holy Spirit in our world! He wrote,

> I beseech you therefore, brethren, by the mercies of God, that you present your bodies a living sacrifice, holy and acceptable to God, which is your reasonable service.
>
> And do not be conformed to this world, <u>but be transformed by the renewing of your mind,</u> that

you may prove what is that good and acceptable and perfect will of God. (Romans 12:1–2)

Christians are expected by God to have lives that are built on the two divine attributes found in transitive truth. We are to have *veracity* and *faithfulness*, just as He does Himself!

Our veracity means that we don't lie, tell "half lies" or "little white lies," or exaggerate or twist the facts when we are describing our successful ventures!

Second, we are people of faithfulness! When we make promises, we keep them. When we enter agreements with others in our world, we can be trusted to talk the talk and walk the walk!

The millennials in our society underlined the importance of several biblical concepts. They valued relationships that were built on authenticity. Genuine Christianity is not a religion but an authentic relationship with the Lord Jesus Christ! The proof of such a testimony is clearly written in large print through our daily lifestyle!

The first level of this transformation impacts our vertical relationship with God Himself. He loves us with a holy agape love that fills our hearts with *joy* and *peace*.

The wonder of redemption is that the God who hates our sin has demonstrated His love for us through the crucifixion and resurrection of His one and only Son (John 3:16; 1 John 3:16; Romans 5:8). It is at Calvary that the penalty for our sin was paid in full. Jesus cried out from the cross, "Tetelesthai," which literally means "Paid in full." He not only paid for our transgressions but also purchased a home for us in heaven!

Let not your heart be troubled, you believe in God, believe also in Me.

In My Father's house are many mansions; if it were not so, I would have told you. I go to prepare a place for you.

And if I go and prepare a place for you, I will come again and receive you unto Myself; that where I am, you shall be also. (John 14:1–3)

The next major consideration is called the transitive love, described in Galatians 5:22 as "longsuffering, kindness and goodness."

This triad of divine love cuts across the excuses we find when someone treats us badly! The usual examples of this statement can be found every day on our highways! We suffer from or witness others who are experiencing road rage! Stories of turning a car into an instrument of retaliation and bullying are reported as the causes of accidents and serious, even life-threatening, injuries!

Domestic abuse occurs from spouse to spouse (male and/or female offenders), from parents to children, and from sibling to sibling!

Our *outward love* is meant to be given to lost souls, our relatives, immediate families, and all of the saints around the world!

Agape love is not extended to someone because of their beauty, worthiness, or kindness! The love is a basic characteristic of knowing the God of love.

1. LONGSUFFERING

The only reason for possessing the character strength called "longsuffering" is that many strangers, friends, relatives and even brothers and sisters in Christ are guilty of verbal, emotional, and even physical abuse!

The critical spirit in many of our churches stands in front of the main entrance into buildings where we worship, pray, serve, and give our tithes and offerings! The number one excuse for not attending church is all the hypocrites who are members! But these are not just found in the pews or theater seats! Quite often the hypocrites are found in our pulpits, preaching one message and living a totally different one!

As though he was anticipating this destructive situation in our generation, Peter raised a question with Jesus.

> Then Peter came to Him and said, "Lord, how often shall my brother sin against me, and I forgive him? Up to seven times?"
>
> Jesus answered him, "I do not say to you, up to seven times, but up to seventy times seven." (Matthew 18:21, 22)

In his First Epistle, the apostle John took this teaching to a deeper application.

Consider 1 John 2:9–11.

> He who says he is in the light, and hates his brother, is in the darkness until now.

He who loves his brother abides in the light, and there is no cause for stumbling in him.

But he who hates his brother is in darkness and walks in darkness, and does not know where he is going, because the darkness has blinded his eyes.

Remember how the "Love Chapter" dealt with these issues in our lives?

Love suffers long and is kind; love does not envy; love does not parade itself, is not puffed up;

Does not behave rudely, does not seek its own, is not provoked, thinks no evil;

Does not rejoice in iniquity, but rejoices in the truth;

Bears all things, believes all things, hopes all things, endures all things.

Love never fails ... (1 Corinthians 13:4–8)

The beauty of this classic passage on love is that it is a word study of the life and ministry of Jesus Christ Himself! He was agape love in human flesh!

The fruit of the Spirit produces a Christlike agape in the hearts and minds of those believers who surrender to the Lordship of Jesus. When He is in charge of your thinking process, you will discover a renewed mind mentioned above (Romans 12:1–2) as the key to having a transformed life.

2. KINDNESS

The second aspect of *transitive love* is found in the fruit of the Spirit listed in Galatians 5:22–23. That aspect is *kindness.*

Kindness places the interests and needs of others ahead of your own. The opposite characteristic is that of selfishness and self-centeredness.

My dad used to spend a lot of time with me discussing the Bible and the problems within our local Baptist church.

On more than one occasion, he would say, *"Son, it's all about selfishness!"*

I would, foolishly, try to argue with him, saying that it was far more complex than such a simple statement.

It's amazing how the foolishness of my dad became wisdom as I grew older! The number one cause of division and strife within the body of Christ is *selfishness!* The apostle Paul would have agreed with Dad! In fact, he said something very close to the same thing that Dad proclaimed to me so long ago.

Romans 6:6

> Knowing this, that our old man (self) was crucified with Him, that the body of sin be done away with, that we should no longer be slaves of sin.

Romans 6:11–14

> Likewise you, also, reckon yourselves to be dead indeed to sin, but alive to God in Christ Jesus our Lord.

Therefore do not let sin reign in your mortal body, that you should obey it in its lusts.

And do not present your members as instruments of unrighteousness to sin, but present yourselves to God as being alive from the dead, and your members as instruments of righteousness to God.

For sin shall not have dominion over you, for you are not under law, but under grace.

3. GOODNESS

The third aspect of the *transitive love* is *goodness*.

The Greek word for goodness is *agathosunay*. "It refers to active goodness as an energetic principle" (Lightfoot, quoted in *Linguistic Key to the Greek New Testament*).

Goodness is agape in action! It is finding a need in someone else and taking the steps to meet that need. It is exercising the gift of helps, encouragement, giving, etc.

Consider what James wrote about this.

If a brother or sister is naked and destitute of daily food,

And one of you says to them, "Depart in peace, be warmed and filled," but you do not give them the things which are needed for the body, what does it profit? (James 2:14–16)

The miracle of spiritual transformation is that God can take the most corrupted minds, cleanse them with the blood of the Lamb, and then transform them through the ministry of the indwelling Holy Spirit!

Paul sent this encouraging message to young Timothy in his second letter:

> Nevertheless the foundation of God stands, having this seal: 'The Lord knows those who are His,' and, 'Let everyone who names the Name of Christ depart from iniquity.'
>
> But in a great house there are not only vessels of gold and silver, but also of wood and clay, some for honor and some for dishonor.
>
> Therefore if anyone cleanses himself from the latter, he will be a vessel for honor, sanctified and useful for the Master, prepared for every good work. (2 Timothy 2:19–21)

A Christian psychologist had just returned from a ministry trip among missionaries overseas and commented, "The only army that shoots its wounded is the Christian army!"

The tragedy of this comment is that it is true! We are plagued with judgmental pharisaism that rejects a brother or sister when they fail to keep our standards of behavior or fundamental theology!

Both behavior and theology are vitally important, but our responsibility before the Captain of our Salvation is to restore the one who has wandered away or fallen into sin! Yet while we are obedient to this divine task, we have been warned to do so in meekness and humility lest we end up in worse condition than the "fallen ones!"

Galatians 6:1 presents us with the principles of restoration.

> Brethren, if a man is overtaken in any trespass, <u>you who
> are spiritual</u> restore such a one in a spirit of gentleness,
> considering yourself lest you also be tempted.

Remember 1 Corinthians 10:12.

> Therefore let him who thinks he stands take heed
> lest he fall!

Verse 13 says,

> No temptation has overtaken you except such as is
> common to man; but God is faithful, Who will not
> allow you to be tempted beyond what you are able,
> but with the temptation will also make the way (John
> 14:6) of escape, that you may be able to bear it.

It may occur to you that this whole subject is *impossible!*

How can anyone change? How can any hopeless addict be set free
from bondage? How can a fallen preacher, missionary, youth leader,
or church member ever be able to serve the Lord again?

It would take a miracle for such a thing to occur!

Yes! That's what I'm talking about! That's what Yahweh explained
to His Old Testament prophet named Ezekiel.

Ezekiel 37:1–3

> The hand of the LORD came upon me and brought
> me out in the Spirit of the LORD, and set me down
> in the midst of the valley; and it was full of bones.

> Then He caused me to pass by them all around, and
> behold, there were many in the open valley; and
> indeed they were very dry.
>
> And He said to me, "Son of man, can these bones
> live?" So I answered, "O LORD God, You know."

Salvation and restoration of a fallen Christian demands the miracle of God's grace! No one can produce the transformation of conversion or revival except for the Spirit of the Living God!

The transitive truth reveals God's *veracity* and *faithfulness.* These divine attributes are found in us in our personal relationship with Him.

The Holy Spirit has saturated us with *love, joy,* and *peace.* These three characteristics of the singular fruit of the Holy Spirit remove terror or timidity in our hearts through our personal fellowship with the Lord. The apostle John testified that God had personally revealed Himself to John through his relationship with Jesus Christ.

On the Mount of Transfiguration, Peter, James, and John were privileged to see and hear the Old Testament prophets Moses and Elijah. They were there to discuss with Jesus the *exodus* (departure) that He would accomplish in a few days.

During this astounding conversation with Jesus, "a bright cloud overshadowed them; and suddenly a voice came out of the cloud, saying 'This is My Beloved Son, in Whom I am well pleased. Hear Him!'" (Matthew 17:1–5).

All three of these disciples made personal references to this staggering encounter with "the King of kings and Lord of lords" in all of His glory.

John wrote,

> That which we have seen and heard we declare to you, that you also <u>may have fellowship with us</u>; and <u>truly our fellowship is with the Father and with His Son Jesus Christ</u>. (1 John 1:3)

The Lord expects His redeemed children to demonstrate both veracity and faithfulness in every part of our relationship with Him! He wants us to be transparent, honest, and humble as we approach Him!

He also wants us to live before our generation in agape love, spiritual joy, and the peace of God that surpasses all understanding and that will guard your hearts, "the seat of affection and love," and minds, "the seat of intellect and mental health."

Cf. 2 Timothy 1:7.

> For God has not given us the spirit of fear (*delia* means "cowardice, timidity, terror"), but of <u>power</u> (*dunamis*, "inherent supernatural power"), <u>love</u> (<u>agape</u>, "divine love"), and of a <u>sound mind</u> (sophronismou, "self-discipline, the power to keep one's self in hand, free from all excitement or hesitation").

The *transitive love* refers to God's attributes of *veracity* and *faithfulness*. He expects all of His children to be truthful in their speech and reliable in their behavior. If you make a promise, then keep it!

The Holy Spirit develops transitive love in us through the three characteristics of the fruit (singular) of the Holy Spirit (Galatians 5:22–23).

As you can clearly see, each of the three groupings of God's transitive attributes has specific areas of impact.

1. The transitive truth establishes a safe and secure relationship between an infinitely holy God and a totally depraved sinner from the human race! This truth defines our *upward relationship with God.*

2. The transitive love reveals God's *mercy* and *goodness* to those who do not deserve it, nor can they earn it in any way! As His children, we too are expected to live out His transitive love through *longsuffering, kindness,* and *goodness.* In these clear commandments, God wants us to reveal transitive love to other people. Some of these friends, neighbors, or relatives are difficult and stretch our patience to a breaking situation.

3. The transitive holiness of God is found in His *justice and righteousness.* The focus for believers in this group of attributes is *an inward application.*

This final grouping of divine attributes will be examined in our next chapter.

THE MASTER'S TOUCH

"Mad Dog" asked me if I would spend some time with him so that he could unload his burden of abuse and brutality endured during his childhood and teens. The damage that was done to Mad Dog produced a serious problem with anger and finding friendship in the streets and in motorcycle gangs.

The day for our lengthy conversation was chosen and the two of us sat in my office at the Peoples Church in Toronto for over four hours! He unleashed the tragedy of his childhood and the violence and abuse endured as a young teenager.

Mad Dog was desperate to receive forgiveness from God and to find a new life promised in the Bible to those who will give their hearts to the Lordship of Jesus Christ! At the end of our lengthy session together, he and I got on our knees by my desk and Mad Dog surrendered his life to "the Master's Touch!"

Our friendship developed over the next months and years as he grew in his Christian life and shared his testimony with many others who were struggling as he did before receiving Jesus as his Savior and Lord! When my wife, Ann, and I left our home in Ontario to become missionaries in Melbourne, Australia, on a four-year contract supported entirely by the Peoples Church.

My role in Melbourne was as the radio pastor and evangelist, in just over three years producing 260 half-hour programs explaining the message of the Bible. These programs were aired into the South Pacific region, where 3.6 billion people lived!

Mad Dog presented me with a gift of an Australian oilskin coat, which I have treasured ever since!

Before we left Toronto, Mad Dog introduced me to a Christian motorcycle club that came to the Peoples Church each summer for a barbecue and an outdoor program including Gospel country music, testimonies, and a message from the chaplain (my privilege). The president of the club explained to the motorcycle guests (including many non-Christian bikers) that the chaplain would move from cycle to cycle to pray with the people who wanted prayer support. Those who chose not to participate were invited to go to the barbecue and get their hamburgers!

To my amazement, I was welcomed at the most of the bikes by the people standing there. In many cases, I had the opportunity to share the good news of Calvary and the resurrected Savior before praying with them!

As I think back over the transformation in the life of Mad Dog, I realize that this man of God was changed because he came under "new control"—the Lordship of Jesus Christ who came to find His lost sheep in a chaotic world!

Chapter Six

A NEW CONTROL

INTRODUCTION

In our previous chapters, we examined the three sections of the communicable or transitive attributes of God. The Lord intends that His children will not only receive a home in heaven, but that they will also receive a personal part in the divine nature of God Himself!

Peter declared that this was the plan of God Himself as He gathered lost souls transforming them into saints! A saint is not so declared as a reward for godly behavior, but godly behavior is the evidence of sainthood received through God's grace!

In chapter 3, we quoted 2 Peter 1:2–4. I've highlighted the portions of this passage that describe the transformation from a sinner to a saint by the grace of God.

> Grace and peace be multiplied to you in the knowledge of God and of Jesus our Lord,
>
> as His divine power has given us all things that pertain to life and godliness, through the knowledge of Him who called us by glory and virtue,

By which have been given to us exceedingly great and precious promises, that through these you may be partakers of the divine nature, having escaped the corruption that is in the world through lust.

The apostle Peter was not providing the foundation for Shirley MacLaine to break out in blaspheme!

In her New Age autobiography titled *Out on a Limb,* she spoke frankly about her belief in reincarnation, meditation, and mediumship. She also described her personal experience on the shore of an ocean when she was prompted to call out in a very loud voice, "I am God! I am God!"

This lie was founded by Lucifer in his rebellion against the Triune God of creation, Providence, and grace!

THE WONDERFUL GRACE OF JESUS!

Over one hundred years ago, hymn writer Haldor Lillenas penned these powerful lyrics:

> Wonderful grace of Jesus, Greater than all my sin;
> How shall my tongue describe it, Where shall its praise begin?
> Taking away my burden, Setting my spirit free,
> For the wonderful grace of Jesus reaches me.

> Wonderful grace of Jesus, Reaching to all the lost,
> By it I have been pardoned, Saved to the uttermost;
> Chains have been torn asunder, Giving me liberty,
> For the wonderful grace of Jesus reaches me.

"Wonderful grace of Jesus, Reaching the most defiled,
By its transforming power Making him God's dear child,
Purchasing peace and heaven For all eternity—
And the wonderful grace of Jesus reaches me.[7]

What is so wonderful about the grace of Jesus? Here are a few items to consider:

- grace for salvation and forgiveness of sins (Ephesians 2:8–9)
- grace for victory over sinful habits (1 Corinthians 10:13; Romans 8:37; 1 Corinthians 15:57)
- grace for fruitful service (John 15:1–5, 16; 1 Corinthians 15:58)
- grace for suffering (2 Corinthians 1:3–7; Romans 8:16–18)
- grace for trials (2 Corinthians 12:7–10)

NOTES

I. The Incarnation of Jesus

The incarnation of Jesus Christ was a miracle predicted seven hundred years before it occurred in the little town of Bethlehem. Isaiah prophesied that a miraculous birth of a baby boy would transform lost souls through the grace of God.

> Therefore the Lord Himself will give you a sign:
> Behold, the virgin shall conceive and bear a Son,
> and shall call His Name Immanuel.

---

[7] Haldor Lillenas, *Praise! Our Songs and Hymns,* "The Wonderful Grace of Jesus" (Singspiration/Zondervan, 1979).

This miraculous virgin birth was announced to Joseph as he struggled with the scandal of his fiancée being with a child! He knew that he was not the father of this baby, because he and Mary were obedient to God's Word, and they were waiting for the completion of their marriage before they had any sexual relationship! Therefore, he could only deduce that Mary had been involved in a sinful relationship with another man!

The angel of the Lord called Gabriel explained the incarnation of Jesus Christ through Joseph's espoused wife, Mary.

> "Joseph, son of David, do not be afraid to take to you Mary your wife, for that which is conceived in her is of the Holy Spirit. And she will bring forth a Son, and you shall call His Name JESUS, for He will save His people from their sins!" (Matthew 1:20–21)

2. The Hypostatic Union

The incarnation of Jesus provided the Son of God with a human body and a human nature (sin excepted). He possessed all of the attributes of the Triune God that were His for all of eternity past, and they were still His in the time of His earthly life, and for all eternity to come thereafter!

Two natures coexisted in His Person known as Jesus. He was entirely human (His favorite title was "the Son of Man"), and at the same time, He was entirely the divine Second Person of the Trinity!

At no time did the two natures possessed by Jesus merge into a hybrid third nature. The two natures coexisted. It was His human being that was "tempted in all points as we are, yet without sin"

(Hebrews 4:15). His humanity was tired, thirsty, scourged, spat upon, abused, crucified, and forsaken by His Father during His crucifixion! It is impossible for the eternal Son of God to die on the cross, but it was essential that the "Second Adam" would be our "Kinsman Redeemer" who would sacrifice Himself to pay the penalty for our sins and to purchase our everlasting home in His Father's dwelling place!

3. The Two Human Natures

When a sinner becomes a saint through the new birth, the new saint discovers that there are two natures in every believer!

One is our old nature, which cannot do anything that is good the eyes of an infinitely holy God! The new nature, which is the indwelling Holy Spirit, can never fall into sin, deceit, and internal corruption!

These two natures living in the bodies of all the saints while on the earth will constantly conduct a spiritual struggle. Spiritual warfare is in the valley of Megiddo located between our ears!

That doesn't deny the full battle of Armageddon, which will take place in the last days of human history, but most of our struggles and failures begin and hold the battle in our own minds! If we could follow that scriptures that speak to us about victorious Christian living, we would rejoice in the grace of God for spiritual warfare!

4. The War within You

In his excellent book *The War within You,* Craig Massey comments on Romans 7.

In order to teach us the truth of the doctrine of two natures and how they oppose each other, God the Spirit has given us a lucid supernatural analysis of our inner conflict in the seventh chapter of Romans. This spectacular portion of Scripture should be studied and perhaps even memorized, for it is basic to the understanding and enjoyment of the Christian life.

There are approximately twenty references to the old nature and twenty references to the new nature in this section. Collectively, the word "I" is used twenty-seven times: sixteen times it designates the action of the new nature, and eleven times it designates the action of the old nature.[8]

Thankfully, Paul did not leave us in the valley of despair but turned the corner in this issue of spiritual warfare when he penned the words of the eighth chapter. He wrote,

There is therefore now no condemnation to those who are in Christ Jesus, who do not walk according to the flesh, but according to the Spirit. (Romans 8:1 NKJV)

5. The Transformation of a Sinner to a Saint

At the end of chapter 5, we left you with a divine plan for our spiritual success and deliverance from the evil one and all his fallen angels known as demons.

---

[8] Craig Massey, *The War within You* (Moody Press, 1987), 82–83.

What we examine now is the third group of divine attributes known as transitive attributes. Just for refreshing our minds, I will share the list we have been considering.

a) The Transitive Truth

The transitive truth attributes are produced in our spiritual walk with God as expressed in Galatians 5:22–23. "But the fruit of the Spirit is love, joy, peace ..."

These three characteristics of Christlikeness describe our upward relationship with our Lord and Savior, Jesus Christ, as well as the Father and the Holy Spirit. So how do we receive these transitive truths?

The process rests on a daily life that is filled with the Holy Spirit! Victory in a Christian's life is not accomplished by making New Year's resolutions or walking up the aisle to the altar to promise God, "Lord, I'll never do that again!"

b) The Transitive Love

The second group of attributes is referred to as *the transitive love* and demonstrates God's mercy and goodness found in His grace. For us, we are instructed to demonstrate His transitive love in our outward relationship with other people. We live in a world that teaches us to look out for number one!

We are called to present the love of God to people who are unlovable! How can we ever sincerely express love to people who criticize us behind our backs or spread rumors about us that are lies and satanic gossip?

The answer lies in our daily walk with the Lord, who lives within our hearts twenty-four/seven!

When the Holy Spirit fills us (play-ro-o), He takes over the control of our thoughts, words, and deeds! This is what the Lordship of Christ is all about!

The love of God mentioned here is the Greek word *agape,* which is a love not based on the appearance of the one we love or their personality, kindness, generosity, flattery, or influence in society! God's love exists because it is a fundamental characteristic of His nature! So too, we must be filled with agape love for others.

c) The Transitive Holiness

The third category of divine transitive attributes is titled the transitive holiness.

The entire list of divine attributes in systematic theology are describe on a foundational truth about Him.

All of His divine attributes are holy attributes. In other words, the wrath of God is holy wrath. The justice of God is equally balanced by His righteousness.

Consider one of the best-loved passages about the Gospel of God's grace.

> For I am not ashamed of the Gospel of Christ, for
> it is the power of God to salvation for everyone who
> believes, for the Jew first and also for the Greek.
>
> For in it the righteousness of God is revealed from faith
> to faith; as it is written, 'The just shall live by faith.'"

For the wrath of God is revealed from heaven against all ungodliness and unrighteousness of men who suppress the truth in unrighteousness,

Because what may be known of God is manifest in them, for God has shown it to them.

For since the creation of the world His invisible attributes are clearly seen, being understood by the things which are made, even His eternal power and Godhead, so that they are without excuse,

Because although they knew God, they did not glorify Him as God, nor were thankful, but became futile in their thoughts, and their foolish hearts were darkened.

Professing to be wise, they became fools,

And changed the glory of the incorruptible God into an image made like corruptible man—and birds and four-footed animals and creeping things.

Therefore God also gave them up to uncleanness, in the lusts of their hearts, to dishonor their bodies among themselves,

Who exchanged the truth of God for the lie, and worshipped and served the creature rather than the Creator, who is blessed forever. Amen." (Romans 1:16–25)

This rebellion against the sovereign and infinitely holy Lord God has produced all manner of social and sexual corruption and condemnation.

For this reason God gave them up to vile passions. For even their women exchanged the natural use for what is against the natural use for what is against nature.

Likewise also the men, leaving the natural use of the woman, burned in their lust for one another, men with men committing what is shameful, and receiving in themselves the penalty of their error which was due.

And even as they did not like to retain God in their knowledge, God gave them over to a debased mind, to do things which are not fitting;

Being filled with all unrighteousness, sexual immorality, wickedness, covetousness, maliciousness, full of envy, murder, strife, deceit, evil-mindedness; they are whisperers,

Backbiters, haters of God, violent, proud, boasters, inventers of evil things, disobedient to parents,

Undiscerning, untrustworthy, unloving, unforgiving, unmerciful;

Who, knowing the righteous justice of God, that those who practice such things, are deserving of death, not only do the same but also approve of those who practice them! (Romans 1:26–32).

The Bible is clear that our God is infinitely holy, and He hates all sin, not just the sins of sexual misbehavior! Furthermore, the Bible is not prejudiced against homosexuality! It is very clear that God hates the heterosexual sins as well!

Any sexual activity outside of the marriage of a man and a woman is condemned as sin!

Sexual intercourse by an unmarried man and woman is called fornication; sexual relationship between two married people who are not husband and wife together is called adultery; sexual relationships between two members of the same sexual identification is called abomination.

Furthermore, Jesus made it clear that we can be guilty of the worst sins without any physical action! Read His application of God's holy judgment.

Matthew 5:21–22

> You have heard it said to those of old, "You shall not murder, and whoever murders will be in danger of the judgment."

> But I say to you that whoever is angry with his brother without a cause shall be in danger of the judgment. And whoever says to his brother "Raca!" shall be in danger of the council. But whoever says "You fool!" shall be in danger of hell fire.

Matthew 5:27–28

> You have heard that it was said to those of old, "You shall not commit adultery."

> But I say to you that whoever looks at a woman to lust for her has already committed adultery in his heart.

The habit of pornographic pictures or movies entails sins of adultery! In fact, many of today's female athletes performing at the Olympics are so scantily dressed that multitudes of men have become dedicated fans of beach volleyball or diving from a board at the diving pool!

THE QUESTION

How can a sinner like you and like me live a life that pleases God and presents a strong personal testimony in a world of desecration and immorality?

In other words, how can a lost sinner be transformed into a saint?

THE ANSWER

Be sure to read part 2, starting next!

THE MASTER'S TOUCH

Pastors are often called upon to assist families that have lost a loved one. While we want to bring comfort to them, we also have the responsibility to share the good news of everlasting life based on the Gospel of Jesus Christ.

After the service was finished in the chapel, I was escorted to the undertaker's car at the front of the processional. I chose to sit in the front seat so that I could chat with the undertaker. This time the undertaker was a young woman in her midforties. Her name was Barb (changed for her privacy).

The procession would travel out of the heart of Toronto to a cemetery nearly forty minutes to the northwest area out of the city.

Over the years, I've made it my custom to ask the undertaker about how they got into this profession and how they felt about it now. Then I asked for permission to ask a searching question about their experience with so many families.

"Would you say that there is a significant difference between families who believe in Jesus Christ and those who do not have such a faith?"

The undertaker looked at me and said, "That's a perceptive question!"

I said, "Yes, it is! What would your answer be?"

She replied, "Without a doubt, the Christian families have peace in spite of their loss, while the others are filled with deep sadness and pain!"

Our conversation took a gentle move from others to her own experience. I received her permission to ask two very personal questions.

"Have you come to the place in your spiritual journey where you *know for certain* that if you were to die today, you would go to heaven?"

Her answer was one I had heard many times in the past!

She said, "Well, I sure hope that I will be allowed to go to heaven! However, I can't say that I am certain! I hope that I will be admitted to such a holy place!"

At this point, I asked her the second question. "Let's assume that you have died and that you are actually speaking to God instead of just me! He met you at the pearly gates and asked you this question: 'Why should I let you into My heaven?' What would your answer be to Him?"

At this crucial part of our conversation, we arrived at the cemetery for the interment!

I asked her if we could continue this talk together after the burial ceremony.

She replied, "Absolutely! I must hear the rest of this discussion!"

The Rest of the Story

When the committal service ended and the cars were leaving the graveyard, she said, "Please continue where we left off! What was that second question again?"

I repeated the second question and waited for her response.

She said, "I have always believed in God and have done my best to live a good life, and I hope that God would let me in! Heaven is a free gift! It is not earned or deserved!"

I walked her through the wonderful grace of Jesus and then asked her, "Barb, does this make sense to you?"

She answered, "Oh yes! It is very clear and straightforward!"

I asked, "Would you like to receive the gift of eternal life?"

She said, "I most certainly would!"

Then she said, "But just a moment. I know the best place for this!"

We soon turned into another cemetery and parked the car in the shade of a great pine tree! Here she prayed a prayer of commitment to Jesus Christ and put her faith in Him alone for salvation!

I am sure that we heard the "Hallelujah Chorus" sung by the angels in heaven!

PART 2

PART 2

Chapter One

PERPLEXITY

INTRODUCTION

During our ministry as the interim pastor at Ulverston Baptist Church in Tasmania, I was asked to lead an adult Bible study on Tuesday evenings.

During the Sunday morning service, the young man leading the worship team decided to promote my adult Bible study on the coming Tuesday evening. As you would expect, he turned to me and said, "Pastor Rush, what is your topic for this Tuesday's Bible study?"

I responded, "Well, brother, I haven't quite decided which title to use, so here are both of them for you: "Why I am no longer a disciple of Jesus!" or "Why I no longer follow Jesus Christ as in the past!"

The leader of the service stood there with a shocked look on his face and said, "Would you please explain this to us?"

I replied, "I will be glad to explain these titles to you this Tuesday evening at 7:00 p.m.!"

That Tuesday evening had a full crowd in the Fellowship Hall!

FUNDAMENTALS

In this chapter, we will consider the New Testament teaching on the concept of discipleship and how this has changed since the birthday of the church of Jesus Christ.

1. The New Creature (2 Corinthians 5:17)

> Therefore, if anyone is in Christ, he is a new creation; old things have passed away; behold all things have become new.

In the devotional booklet called *Our Daily Bread*, Con Campbell made the following comment on August 2, 2021:

> In Jesus, believers are made "children of God" through faith in Him (Galatians 3:26). We're adopted by God and become His sons and daughters (4:5). As God's adopted children, we receive the Spirit of His Son, we call Him "Father" (vs. 6), and we become His heirs (vs. 7) and coheirs with Christ (Romans 8:17). We become full members of His family.[9]

Yahweh made it clear to Israel that He would make a "New Covenant" with those who place their faith in His Son, the Messiah and Anointed One named Jesus Christ! This New Covenant described the internalization of what had been taught to the Jews for many generations!

---

[9] Con Campbell, *Our Daily Bread* (Grand Rapids, Michigan: Our Daily Bread Ministries).

Ezekiel 36:26, 27

> I will give you a new heart and put a new spirit within you; I will take the heart of stone out of your flesh and give you a heart of flesh.

> I will put My Spirit within you and cause you to walk in My statutes, and you will keep My judgments and do them.

This new covenant is explained in the New Testament in Hebrews 8:7–13.

2. The Disciples

Have you ever wondered why the disciples of our Lord were so *perplexed?*

Simon Peter

Simon Peter spoke quickly when the Lord asked the disciples who they though that He was (Matthew 16:16–17).

> Simon Peter answered and said, "You are the Christ (Anointed One), the Son of the Living God."

> Jesus answered and said to him, "Blessed are you, Simon Bar-Jonah, for flesh and blood has not revealed this to you, but My Father Who is in heaven."

Simon Peter spoke quickly shortly thereafter when Jesus revealed to them that He must go to Jerusalem and suffer many things from the elders, chief priests, and scribes and be killed and be raised on the third day.

> Simon took Jesus aside and rebuked Him, saying "Far be it from You, Lord; this shall not happen to You!"

> Jesus turned and said to Peter: "Get behind Me, Satan! You are an offense to Me, and you are not mindful of the things of God, but the things of men!" (Matthew 16:22–23)

The Disciples as a Group

For three and a half years, His disciples were with Jesus twenty-four/seven and listened to His sermons, lessons, and responses to His hecklers among the religious leaders. But the disciples were not able for them to understand His parables. (See Matthew 13:10, 36.)

Of the twelve disciples later called apostles, Judas Iscariot betrayed Jesus for thirty pieces of silver, and Peter denied that he knew Christ three times before the rooster crowed, as Jesus had predicted!

On that terrible night of His arrest, all of His disciples fled into the darkness lest they would be identified as the followers of Jesus Christ, the Messiah!

The disciples were all as guilty as "the doubting Thomas!" While Thomas required evidence on which he could establish his faith in the resurrection of Jesus, the others also could not accept the truth of the Lord's resurrection. They could not believe in His crucifixion, His burial in Joseph of Arimathea's new tomb, and His resurrection on the third day as He predicted to them!

What is the explanation of the failure of these prayerfully selected followers of the Son of God? Here are several suggestions:

1. Unsaved people cannot overcome their fallen natures.
2. No amount of teaching can cause an unredeemed sinner to become godly.
3. The standards of Christ were unattainable through discipleship.
4. Discipleship was a temporary stepping-stone between the Old Testament and the New Testament post-Pentecost church.

The disciples needed to experience the new birth as Jesus explained to Nicodemus. Sincere Judaism was not enough to see or enter the kingdom of heaven! The Spirit of the New Covenant had not taken up residence inside the bodies of the disciples until the Day of Pentecost in the upper room!

3. The Word Study

The Greek word for disciple is *mathetes*. It occurs 232 times in the four Gospels and twenty-seven times in the first part of the book of Acts. Its last usage in the New Testament is in Acts 21:16, and it does not occur in the epistles or the book of Revelation. The Hebrew word for disciple is *limmud*, but it is not mentioned in the Old Testament.

The standard for someone to become a disciple is that he would dedicate himself to twenty-four/seven living with his master so that he could spend as much time as possible observing the master's actions and reactions and that he could listen to the master's teaching/preaching and responses to his critics. As a disciple, this student was expected to ask the master questions.

The twelve disciples of Jesus Christ were His apostles because they were called to be sent on special missions and service.

In addition to these twelve selected disciples, there was a group of seventy disciples assigned to carry the message of the kingdom of God into the villages. For this particular ministry, the Holy Spirit came upon these seventy servants and granted them the power to heal the sick, deliver those under demonic oppression, and other forms of deliverance. Some would say that these seventy men were born again because the Spirit came upon them. In contrary to this conclusion, we know that the Holy Spirit had a very amazing ministry during the Old Testament days, but He never took up residence inside the bodies of the believers!

In fact, King David repented of his sins of adultery, murder, and deception after the prophet called Nathan rebuked him for his gross corruption! His repentance is written in Psalm 51 in which he made a plea with the Lord in verse 11 that does not apply to New Testament born-again believers!

Psalm 51:11

> Do not cast me away from Your presence, and do not take Your Holy Spirit from me.

John 14:16–18

> And I will pray the Father, and He will give you another (literally "another of the same kind") Helper, that He may abide with you forever—

> The Spirit of Truth, Whom the world cannot receive, because it neither sees Him nor knows Him; but you know Him, for He dwells with you, and will be in you.

I will not leave you orphans; I will come to you.

The word *mathetes (disciple)* appears in the New Testament for the last time in Acts 21:16.

QUESTION

Why was the word *disciple* no longer used in the New Testament?

ANSWERS

- The primary function of a disciple was to dwell in the presence of the Master twenty-four/seven, but the Master was going to leave them (John 14:16–18 as above).
- The disciples were instructed to wait in the upper room until the Father sent them another (of the same kind) Helper.
- The plan of the Lord for the building of His church involved Peter in the early stages (Acts 1–12) and Paul (Acts 13–28) in the missionary period.

THE ACTS OF THE APOSTLES

The book of Acts is focused on two major apostles. Acts 1–12 describes Peter's ministry, and Acts 13–28 covers the missionary ministry of the apostle Paul.

PETER'S INSTRUCTIONS (MATTHEW 16:18–19)

And I also say to you that you are Peter, and on this rock I will build My Church, and the gates of Hades shall not prevail against it.

And I will give you the keys of the kingdom of heaven, and whatever you bind on the earth will have been bound in heaven (margin, literal translation), and whatever you loose on earth will have been loosed in heaven (margin, literal translation).

The keys of the kingdom of heaven were simply the Gospel presentation in the power of the Holy Spirit.

Acts 1:8

But you shall receive power when the Holy Spirit has come upon you; and you shall be witnesses to Me in Jerusalem, and in all Judea and Samaria, and to the end of the earth.

THE FIVE STAGES OF THE GROWTH OF THE CHURCH

1. The Ministry of Peter

Acts 2:1–4 tells us about the 120 disciples who were hiding in the upper room with the doors locked because they were afraid of the Jews! I heard a pastor recently stating that these disciples were faithfully meeting in the upper room for prayer that produced the coming of the Holy Spirit! Not so! These fearful disciples were baptized by the Holy Spirit into the body of Christ in the upper room. In holy boldness, they left the safety of the room and proclaimed the Gospel of Jesus Christ to the Jews gathered in Jerusalem from all parts of the world! (Peter used the keys of the kingdom of heaven along with the

120 disciples who were hiding in the upper room and then were filled with the Holy Spirit!)

Three thousand unbelieving Jewish men became believers in Jesus and were baptized into the body of Christ by the indwelling Holy Spirit (Acts 2:40–47). In the Old Testament, we find that the birthday of Israel took place on the Day of Pentecost, and they received the Law of God, but three thousand unbelieving Jews were slain because of their gross corruption, sin, and rebellion against Yahweh! (Peter opened the door of the kingdom to unbelieving Jews as the Holy Spirit opened their eyes to the Gospel! The three thousand Jewish converts were men, but there were ladies and children as well!)

The hated Samaritans were led to faith in Jesus by the Jewish disciples, and they were welcomed into the fellowship of the saints (Acts 8:4–8, 14–25)! The body of Christ was created by the Spirit of God through the new birth (John 3:3–21). Now the Samaritan and Jewish believers became saints and brothers and sisters by the wonderful grace of Jesus! (Peter used the keys of the kingdom of heaven to welcome the hated Samaritans into the body of Christ!)

This is the powerful story of the Lord sending Peter to share the Gospel with Cornelius and his family, even though they were Gentiles—dogs in the minds of the Jewish people! Peter even argued with the Lord when he was shown a great sheet filled with all kinds of animals. Notice how the Lord used Peter's situation.

Acts 10:9–16

> The next day, as they went on their journey and
> drew near the city, Peter went up on the housetop
> to pray, about the sixth hour.
>
> Then he became very hungry and wanted to eat,
> but while they made ready, he fell into a trance ...

While in the trance Peter was shown this large sheet full of animals, including those that were listed as unclean and forbidden by the laws of the Old Testament. The Lord then said to him, "Rise, Peter; kill and eat!"

Now consider Peter's response to His Lord.

> But Peter said, "Not so, Lord! For I have never eaten
> anything common or unclean!"

Verse 15: "And a voice spoke to him the second time, 'What God has cleansed you must not call common!'"

This was done three times. And the object was taken up into heaven again. Three men arrived at Peter's place of rest, sent by Cornelius as led by the Holy Spirit. At this time, the Holy Spirit informed Peter that three men were seeking for him and that he should go down and go with them to a Gentile home.

The Gospel of Jesus was proclaimed to a houseful of the family, their friends, and neighbors, and the Gentiles were baptized by the Spirit into the body of Christ! Many of us today are born-again Christians, even though we were part of pagan Gentiles in our family trees! (Peter was used by the Holy Spirit to open the door to pagan Gentiles so that they, too, could be forgiven of all their sins and to be baptized by the Holy Spirit into the body of Christ!)

2. The Missionary Ministry of the Apostle Paul

Paul's instructions in Acts 9:15–16: Ananias is encouraged by the Lord so that he would do "follow-up visitation" with Saul of Tarsus!

The ministry of Paul included evangelizing twelve disciples of John the Baptist.

These men, who were dedicated to the forerunner, John the Baptist, were led by Paul to salvation in Christ, were baptized in water, and then were baptized by the Holy Spirit into the body of Christ (Acts 19:1–7).

Paul asked these men a very crucial question.

> Did you receive the Holy Spirit when you believed?
> (Acts 19:2)

They replied, "We have not so much as heard whether there is a Holy Spirit!"

Paul explained the Gospel of Jesus to these men, and they received Him as their Savior! They were then baptized in water. Paul laid his hands on them, the Holy Spirit came upon them, and they were baptized into the body of Christ!

3. The Missionary Service Begins

The church in Antioch (where believers in Christ were first called "Christians") prayed and separated Paul and Barnabas as full-time missionaries. The missionary journeys of Paul are recorded in the second half of the book of Acts.

The ministry of evangelism was not limited to just the apostles! Everyone who belonged to the church of Jesus was called by God to witness the good news to the lost souls covering the world!

1 Peter 2:9, 10

> But you are a chosen generation, a royal priesthood, a holy nation, His own special people, that you may proclaim the praises of Him who called you out of darkness into His marvelous light;

> Who once were not a people but are now the people of God, who had not obtained mercy but now have obtained mercy.

4. Discipleship

This word so often used among our church leaders does not exist in the Bible. Why? Because we are not commanded to pursue other believers for the purpose of discipling them!

Furthermore, the disciples of Jesus were a long way from the foundation of the church that they would become!

In his devotional booklet, Charles Stanley has this to say about the disciples:

> Even after three years in Jesus' company, the disciples couldn't live the Christian life on their own. They had to wait for the indwelling Holy Spirit, who gave them strength, guidance, and wisdom. That has not changed—it remains true that apart from Christ's Spirit, we cannot overcome fleshly desires and live

in obedience to God's will. But when we rely on Him instead of ourselves, He produces godly desires within us, empowers obedience, and transforms our character into Christ's likeness[10]

This comment is also expressed by John MacArthur Jr.

The apostles themselves obviously lacked the understanding and spiritual power to complete Jesus' unfinished ministry of evangelism and edification. However, in these last words to them before His ascension, the Lord Jesus Christ reiterates (cf. John 20:22) the promise of the Spirit. He will empower the apostles (and all subsequent believers) with those resources necessary to finish the Savior's unfinished work. They needed the correct message, manifestation, might, mystery, mission, and motive.[11]

The disciples of Jesus were in transition between the Old Testament and the New Testament. They had not received the Holy Spirit as would occur on the Day of Pentecost. The "birthday of the church" was based on the indwelling of the Spirit of Christ, and He would never leave the believer for all of eternity!

5. The Great Commission

There have been a few people who have read the original manuscript for this book who have asked this question: "Doesn't the great

---

[10] Charles Stanley, *In Touch Devotional Booklet,* March 11, 2021, 16.
[11] John MacArthur Jr., *The MacArthur New Testament Commentary, Acts 1–12, 11* (Chicago: Moody Press, 1964).

commission command that we are expected to make disciples all over the world?"

This is a good question! This requires a good answer!

Considering the Matthew version of the great commission, let's practice exegesis.

Matthew 28:18–20

> All authority has been given to Me in heaven and on earth.
>
> Go therefore and make disciples of all the nations, baptizing them in the Name of the Father, and of the Son, and of the Holy Spirit,
>
> Teaching them to observe all things that I have commanded you; and lo, I am with you always, even to the end of the age.

OBSERVATIONS

The great commission is predicated on the sovereign authority of Jesus Christ throughout both heaven and earth.

The orders from Jesus are based on four different words.

A) "Go" (poreuthaysan). The first participle is an aorist participle and implies that the Lord's disciples will be going to the ends of the world on His plan!

Acts 1:8

> But you shall receive power when the Holy Spirit
> has come upon you; and you shall be witnesses to
> Me in Jerusalem, and in all Judea, and Samaria, and
> to the end of the earth." "Now Saul was consenting
> to his death (Stephen, the church's first martyr).
> At that time a great persecution arose against the
> church which was at Jerusalem; and they were
> all scattered throughout the regions of Judea and
> Samaria, except the apostles.

Acts 8:4

> Therefore those who were scattered went everywhere
> preaching the Word.

Their going from Jerusalem to the ends of the earth was part of the
plan of the Lord!

The great commission also contains two more participles and one
imperative to examine.

B) "Make disciples of all the nations" *(mathayteusate)*. This command
is in the aorist, imperative. It means this command is to be obeyed
completely with a punctiliar action. In other words, this is not a
continuous program called discipleship, but it is the presentation of
the Gospel to an unbeliever.

H. E. Dana and Julius R. Mantey, the authors of the textbook *A
Manual Grammar of the Greek New Testament,* wrote,

> There are really two fundamental ways of viewing
> action. It may be contemplated is single perspective,

as a point, which we may call <u>punctiliar</u> action; or it may be regarded as in process, as a line, and this we may call <u>linear</u> action.[12]

To further clarify this statement, the authors provided us with an illustration concerning the aorist, imperative tense.

The aorist may be represented by a dot (.), the present by a line (_____).[13]

This grammatical study makes it clear that the commandment to make disciples of all the nations is referring to a completed presentation of the Gospel to a lost soul, resulting in that person surrendering to the Lordship of Jesus Christ and becoming new creations in a moment of time!

Remember 2 Corinthians 5:17.

Therefore, if anyone is in Christ, he is a new creation; old things have passed away, behold, all things have become new.

1 Corinthians 2:14

But the natural man does not receive the things of the Spirit of God, for they are foolishness to him; nor can he know them, because they are spiritually discerned.

The disciples of Jesus did not experience this conversion, new birth, re-creation, etc., until the Day of Pentecost.

---

[12] H. E. Dana and Julius R. Mantey, *A Manual Grammar of the Greek New Testament*, 179.
[13] Ibid., 179.

The great commission included two other present participles.

C) Baptizing *(baptizontes)* (a present participle) means "continue baptizing them in the name of the Father, and of the Son, and of the holy Spirit."

D) Teaching *(didaskontes)* (a present participle) means "continue teaching them to keep, observe, obey, all that Jesus had commanded."

Please note: This term is not the teaching process found in academia or in theological postgraduate instruction! This is leading new believers to the place where they are obedient to the Lordship of Christ!

The ministry of the disciples would transfer into the ministry of sainthood as the church of Jesus Christ fulfilled His prophecy that they would become His witnesses, and the Gospel would spread in Jerusalem, Judea, Samaria, and to the uttermost parts of the world!

Our next chapter will unpack this phenomenal use of the "keys of the kingdom of heaven" allowing pagans to become the children of God!

THE MASTER'S TOUCH

My teacher in soul winning was a fine gentleman named Jim. He took me to the corner of Jarvis and Gerrard streets in Toronto to witness to customers at the Keystone Bar. As they came out of the bar, we would hand them a Gospel tract and try to carry on a conversation.

On this night, it had been raining fairly hard and there were puddles along the sidewalk. When two men came out of the bar, they were staggering under the influence of the alcohol. One of them resented me because I was a teenager holding my Bible in my hand. He swore at me and took a swing at my head, but he missed and knocked my Bible into a puddle of water!

His companion swore at him and said, "You should never hit a man of God!" He then picked up my Bible and dried it off on his shirt. He apologized for the damage to the Bible and my tracts. He was a man who walked with a cane and was stooped over with a bad back, but he bent over to pick up my things out of the mud!

Jim and I took him across the street to a restaurant and bought him some coffee and food. As we sat there, we heard his story.

He said that his name Mickie Walker, but he was known in Detroit as "Michigan Mickie Walker." He had a very successful career as a musician in a band that played in a number of nightclubs. He was often treated with ale and beer by the customers who enjoyed his music. Their generosity led Mickie to alcoholism, and he gradually lost his skill in music. And he lost his job and then his family when his wife left him with their children! Mickie crossed the border into Windsor, hitchhiked to Toronto, and found a room in a flophouse on Pembroke Street. It was a notorious and large rooming house for drunkards and those on drugs.

We were able to visit Mickie several times, but Jim and I were concerned that we had not seen him for quite some time. We went to his rooming house, but the landlord stopped us and said, "Please break into his room and see if he is OK!" We replied, "No, sir! You have the keys, so you open the door and we'll go in for you!"

When we entered Mickie's room, we were almost made nauseous by the smell and filth that covered his bed, his pajamas, the floor, and the chair. He had been sick many times and was lying on the bed unconscious.

Jim and I set about to clean up the mess, put clean sheets on the bed, wash him, and dress him in clean pajamas. Then Jim said, "I'm going to read from John 3, and then would you pray for him, asking the Lord to heal him from this terrible bondage to booze?"

We both prayed and asked the Lord to set him free and to bring him back to consciousness. We were exhausted at this point, so we quietly left him resting on his bed.

About two or three weeks later, we were walking along Gerrard Street and saw a well-dressed and strong-looking man walking the other way. As we passed him, he called out, "What? Are you stuck up? Won't you say hello to an old friend?"

To our amazement, it was Michigan Mickie Walker, who was sober, clean, dressed in a suit, and walking without his cane—or even being bent over! The Lord had saved him when we prayed, because he was conscious and prayed in his heart for forgiveness and healing!

The sequel to this story was the restoration of his marriage, and he was welcome in their new home in Detroit! His new life in Christ was permanent!

Chapter Two

PENTECOST

INTRODUCTION

Pentecost comes from the Greek language and means "fiftieth day." It was the Feast of the Firstfruits held fifty days after the Feast of Passover.

ITEM 1

On April 14, 1491 BC, the fathers in the homes of the Israelites living as slaves in Egypt offered the Passover Lamb and placing the blood on the door sides and the lintel so that the death angel would pass them by and spare their firstborn sons.

Fifty days later, Israel was located at the feet of Mount Sinai during the first week of June.

This special day was chosen by God for the birthday of Israel as a nation under His divine authority. This occurred when Moses was alone with Yahweh on Mount Sinai. The entire nation of Jews was drawn to the foot of this mountain and kept from the intense holiness of God's presence on the top. They were terrified with the flames, smoke, and earthquakes. That was an object lesson that no one could approach the Lord God until his or her sins were atoned and forgiven.

On that amazing day two men were in the upper region with God. Moses and his brother Aaron were invited to meet with the Lord face-to-face! These two men returned down the mountain to prepare the people of Israel for worship and service of the infinitely holy God named Yahweh.

When this was completed, the Lord called Moses to come up to Him again, but this time by himself. Aaron was to stay with the Jews to keep them in a state of worship. Moses would stay up on the mountain for forty days as he received the entire Pentateuch (Genesis to Deuteronomy), including the following three categories of the laws in the Mosaic Covenant:

- the moral code (the Ten Commandments)
- the spiritual code including the seven *Levitical feasts* and the five *Levitical offerings*
- the social code containing the regulations for Israel's diet, sanitation, quarantine, soil conservation, taxation, military service, marriage, childbirth, divorce, etc.

One of the Ten Commandments is the institution of the keeping of the Sabbath.

The first time the term "Sabbath" is found in the Bible is in Exodus 16:23. For 2,500 years, no one on earth observed the Sabbath day—just the Lord in heaven (Genesis 2:2)!

- The Sabbath was to Israel (Exodus 31:13, 17), who knew nothing about it until this event.
- The Sabbath was never given to the church of Christ (Colossians 2:16; Galatians 4:9–11).

- "Sabbath" does not mean "seven" but "rest" or "cessation."
- There were many Sabbaths given to Israel, including the following:
  - the weekly Sabbath
  - the first day of the seventh month
  - the tenth day of the seventh month (the Day of Atonement)
  - the fifteenth day of the seventh month (Feats of Tabernacles)
  - the seventh year for the land to be idle for one whole year
  - the fiftieth-year Sabbath with the trumpet sounding the jubilee year

When Moses descended from the top of the mountain, carrying the Ten Commandments on two stone copies, he discovered a tragedy! The huge crowd had enlisted Aaron to gather their jewels, gold, and silver, melt them down, and form a calf that they could then worship! When Aaron produced this idol, the people had a party, and many of them were drunk and immoral in their behavior!

Moses was filled with righteous wrath, to the extent that he threw the Ten Commandments on the ground; the stone tablets were shattered into small pieces! Furthermore, God took three thousand unbelieving Jewish men from this life into eternity in hell!

Item 2

Fifty days after the Passover, the second major Day of Pentecost occurred. During the first forty post-Resurrection days, the Lord made many appearances to His disciples, even meeting with five hundred disciples at one time, proving that He was alive in the same body that was crucified and buried in a tomb. A huge, one-and-a-half-ton rock covered the door, sealed by Rome for security so that no disciples could steal His body away!

At the conclusion of His appearances, Jesus ascended from the earth to His Father's throne in glory!

Acts 1:9–11

> Now when He had spoken these things (about the coming of the Holy Spirit to empower His disciples and to introduce His church), while they watched, He was taken up, and a cloud received Him out of their sight (possibly the Shekinah glory cloud).
>
> While they looked steadfastly toward heaven as He went up, behold, two men stood by them in white apparel,
>
> Who also said, "Men of Galilee, why do you stand gazing up into heaven? This same Jesus, who was taken up into heaven, will so come in like manner as you have seen Him go into heaven."

When the disciples left the site of the ascension of the Lord, they went to Jerusalem and entered the upper room as instructed by the Lord when He told them His Father's promise would be fulfilled. They would receive the Holy Spirit in a way they had never experienced before!

You may be wondering about the time when the Holy Spirit empowered the seventy disciples as they obeyed the Master's command to travel through the towns and villages, preaching the message of the kingdom of God.

Luke 10:1

> After these things the Lord appointed seventy others
> also, and sent them two by two before His face into
> every city and place where He Himself was about to
> go. (See verses 2–24 for the whole story.)

These seventy disciples were granted the presence and power of the Holy Spirit on a temporary basis so that they could prepare the way for the Messiah to follow them up in those same cities. Their experience was the same as those recorded in the Old Testament in which the Spirit of God came upon human beings to provide them with protection, power, and liberty in His service.

At this earlier experience, the disciples were not indwelt by the Holy Spirit, which occurs at conversion!

Ten days following His post-Resurrection appearances, He kept His Father's promise and sent the Holy Spirit to take up permanent home in the 120 disciples in the upper room. The signs of the Holy Spirit's ministry to the disciples were astounding!

- The sudden sound of a mighty wind rushed in from heaven and filled the whole house where they met.
- All the disciples in the room discovered tongues of flames hovering over their heads!
- Everyone experienced the filling of the Holy Spirit as He took up permanent residence within each believer's body.
- The entire baby church of Christ was blessed with the miracle of speaking in the languages and dialects of the multitudes of Jews who were in Jerusalem to celebrate the Feast of Firstfruits. The gift of tongues was provided for evangelism, not proving to other believers that you have been "baptized in the Holy Spirit!" The gift of glossolalia

was an ability not obtained through studies, practice, and guidance from an expert! In some way of looking at this phenomenon, this was also a miracle of hearing as it was of speaking.

1 Corinthians 6:19, 20

> Or do you not know that your body is the temple (naos) of the Holy Spirit who is in you, whom you have from God, and you are not your own?
>
> For you were bought with a price; therefore glorify God in your body and in your spirit, which are God's.

The Holy Spirit directed Paul's choice of using the Greek word *naos* instead of *hieron*, which includes every part of the temple, including the ground on which it has been built.

Instead, the Holy Spirit chose the word *naos* because it specifically refers to the Holy of Holies, behind the veil that was torn in two from the top to the bottom at the exact moment when Jesus died on the cross!

Christians walk all over our world as living places where the Shekinah glory of God called home!

THE BAPTISM OF THE HOLY SPIRIT

Here's a study that I learned many years ago. I wanted to examine every NT reference to the Baptism of the Holy Spirit. The outcome of that research is below.

The Baptism of the Holy Spirit

Predicted

Matthew 3:11; Mark 1:8; Luke 3:16; 24:49; John 1:33; Acts 1:4, 8

Fulfilled

Acts 2:1–11; 8:14–17 (no tongues); 10:44–48; 11:15–17; 15:6–9; Acts 19:1–7

Explained

1 Corinthians 12:3

At conversion we receive five ministries of the Holy Spirit.

1. He regenerates us (Titus 3:5; John 3:3–7; 1 Peter 1:23; James 1:18).
2. He baptizes us (Romans 6:3–4; 1 Corinthians 12:13; Galatians 3:27; Ephesians 4:4–5; Colossians 2:12).
3. He seals us (2 Corinthians 1:22; Ephesians 1:14–16; 4:30; 2 Corinthians 1:22; 5:5).
4. He indwells us (John 14:16, 20; 7:37–39; 1 Corinthians 2:12; 3:16; Romans 8:9).
5. He fills us (Acts 2:4; 4:8; 6:3; 7:55; 9:17; 13:9; 13:52; Ephesians 5:18; Galatians 5:16).

The five ministries all occur at the moment of our salvation. The first four are permanent and need never to be prayed for or experienced as a second blessing after conversion. The four ministries mentioned here cannot be lost or taken away from you because of sin and spiritual backsliding!

The fifth ministry can be lost and requires a daily, even a moment-by-moment, commandment to be obeyed! Filling really means surrender to the Lordship of Jesus in all areas of your life!

Ephesians 5:18

> And do not be drunk with wine, in which is dissipation; but be filled with the Spirit.

The word translated as "filled" is play-ro-o, which means "controlled."

The *Linguistic Key to the Greek New Testament* explains this meaning for us.

> The idea of the word is "control." The indwelling Spirit of God is the One who should continually control and dominate the life of the believer.

GRAMMATICAL LESSON

- The tense: the present tense means that this should be continuous.
- The mood: as an imperative mood, this is not an option to be considered but a commandment to be obeyed.
- The voice: the verb is in the passive voice, which means that we surrender to the Spirit; we are not doing anything to bring this to our lives.
- The number: the verb is in the plural number, signifying that this commandment is for all believers!

Play-ro-o has been used in Greek literature in three ways.

1. The control is illustrated by the wind filling the sails of a boat and enabling it to move across the body of water that it's in.
2. The control is like the impact of salt on beef. The salt permeates the meat so that all of it roasts with a delicious flavor.
3. The control is illustrated as one being is in authority over another person. It also is seen in demonization when evil spirits take control of a human being!

THE PRESENCE OF GOD

As a young pastoral student many years ago, I was taught by a senior pastor that we need to pray the "Invocation" at the beginning of the church service. In this prayer, we are asking the Lord to be with us during our worship, praise, and prayer time. We would say something like this: "We come into Your presence in the name of Your Son, the Lord Jesus Christ."

The Old Testament would find this prayer to be appropriate, but the post-Pentecost believers were called "saints" who possessed the presence of the Lord twenty-four/seven!

THE POWER OF GOD

Dr. Oswald J. Smith, the missionary statesman and founder of the Peoples Church, Toronto, was also a writer of a multitude of poems, hymns, and books for Christians that have been translated into a host of languages and provided as a gift to missionaries around the world. I had the tremendous privilege of having my office at the Peoples Church right beside OJ Smith!

We had many conversations and prayers at the beginning of a day of ministry. He also made sure that I received most of his books for my own blessing and growth!

In his book titled *The Enduement of Power,* he wrote,

> And let me say that it is not a question of our getting more of the Holy Spirit, but rather of the Holy Spirit getting more of us! We allow Him to occupy one or two of the rooms, but we do not hand over the key and give Him access to every part. He must possess all for He is not the guest, but the Head of the home![14]

VICTORY IN CHRIST

An unknown Christian wrote two books: one on prayer and the other on Christian victory titled *How to Live the Victorious Life.* In it, he or she wrote,

> Jesus Christ has won the victory for us. "I live" says Paul, "yet not I, Christ liveth in me."
>
> So we come back to the same theme: The secret of Victory is the indwelling Christ. Victory is in trusting, not in trying. "This is the victory that overcomes the world"—and sin—"even our faith" (1 John 5:4).[15]

---

[14] Oswald J. Smith, *The Enduement of Power,* 24.
[15] An unknown Christian, *How to Live the Victorious Life,* 23.

Galatians 2:20

> I have been crucified with Christ; it is no longer I who live, but Christ lives in me, and the life which I now live in the flesh I live by faith in the Son of God, who loved me and gave Himself for me.

1 John 1:7–9

> But if we walk in the light as He is in the light, we have fellowship with one another, and the blood of Jesus Christ, His Son, cleanses (keeps on cleansing—present tense) from all sin.

> If we say that we have no sin, we deceive ourselves, and the truth is not in us.

> If we confess our sins, He is faithful and just to forgive us our sins, and to cleanse us from all unrighteousness.

WALKING AS A BELIEVER IN EPHESIANS

Ephesians 4:1   "Walk worthy of the calling with which you were called …"

Ephesians 4:17   "That you should no longer walk as the rest of the Gentiles, in the futility of their mind …"

Ephesians 5:2   "And walk in love (agape), as Christ also has loved us and given Himself for us …"

| Ephesians 5:8 | "For you were once darkness, but now you are light in the Lord. Walk as children of light …" |
| Ephesians 5:15 | "Seen then that you walk circumspectly, not as fools but as wise, redeeming the time, because the days are evil." |

THE TRANSITION

1. The disciples were doing their best to think like, speak like, act like, and react like the Master, the Lord Jesus Christ! But they could not reach that level of holiness. Furthermore, they could not understand His parables, His decisions, and His responses to the scribes and Pharisees who tried to catch Him in an error!

2. First Corinthians 2:14 explains their blindness, deafness, and confusion over spiritual truths.

> But the natural man does not receive the things of the Spirit of God, for they are foolishness to him; nor can he know them, because they are spiritually discerned.

3. Why didn't Jesus simply redeem His disciples and allow them to possess the indwelling Spirit to illuminate them?

Answer: Jesus could not save anyone until He had died on the cross. The first convert to the Gospel was the thief who was dying on the cross beside Jesus! Remember that Jesus gave him a delayed promise! He said, "Assuredly, I say to you, today you will be with Me in Paradise!"

Within a few more hours both men had died on their crosses, and both of them rejoiced in their heavenly home.

As observed previously, the word "disciple" *ceased being used in the New Testament from Acts 21:16.* Why? Not because their failure to understand the teaching and preaching of the Lord, resulting in the removal of disciples totally, but that this role was advanced to a higher position.

The twelve disciples who were chosen by Jesus after a whole night of prayer became known as the apostles (excluding Judas Iscariot, who was replaced in Acts 1:15–26 by Matthias).

THE TRANSFORMATION

The disciples of Jesus, excluding Judas Iscariot, were baptized by the Spirit into the body of Christ, and the Godhead took up permanent residence within their bodies and souls! The fearful followers of the Lord were empowered to leave the upper room and proclaim the Gospel to the unbelieving Jews that had come from all over the world to be in attendance in Jerusalem for the Feast of Firstfruits.

Three thousand unbelieving Jewish men came to life and to receive the gift of salvation through faith in their Messiah, whose name was Jesus! The New Testament church grew in massive numbers: 120 in the upper room evangelized in Jerusalem and three thousand unbelieving Jewish men were converted to faith in Jesus Christ alone for salvation.

The Lord added to the church every day as the crowds of people were saved through His death, burial, and resurrection. As Peter and John continued preaching the Gospel, the number in Jerusalem grew to five thousand men (Acts 4:4)!

As this movement of the Holy Spirit touched thousands of hearts, the numbers were no longer added to the church but multiplied, including both men and women (Acts 5:14). The number of disciples was multiplied greatly (Acts 6:1), and even a great number of Jewish priests "were obedient to the faith!" (Acts 6:7).

When Paul returned to Jerusalem from his missionary trips, he observed the many thousands of believers who were all zealous in keeping the laws of God in their new faith in Christ (Acts 21:20).

In our next chapter, we'll examine the new terminology applied to the disciples (and apostles), all of the crowds of disciples that followed Jesus, and the believers that came to Christ through the ministry of the writing called the New Testament!

THE MASTER'S TOUCH

My sister's friend was a tough and worldly businesswoman who was very quick with her arguments about virtually everything!

She covered her facial features with hard and strong colors of makeup, giving everyone the impression that she was beyond sharing the Gospel with her!

She became a friend of my oldest sister since they worked together in the head office of a main department store in downtown Toronto. Iona was able to invite her to come to the morning service at our church and then travel out to Streetsville some twenty-five miles for a midday dinner with the family.

She not only accepted the invitation, but she came back to Toronto that evening for the evening service! While she was in our home, she argued with our dad frequently and was not shy about using cursing and rude expressions. Dad would tell her that her language made her look ignorant and vulgar!

After a series of Sunday evening services, she surprised every one of us at the end of the closing hymn. Without an altar call to receive Christ, she walked down to the front, and a lady who was on the church's counseling team came down to stand beside her.

Iona's friend and the lady counselor went through the back room to a private office. Here this lady led her through a clear presentation of the Gospel of Jesus and to a personal commitment to Jesus!

After nearly an hour, the two ladies came out of the office, and we had a hard time in recognizing her! Her face was cleaned from the hard makeup, and her countenance was amazingly transformed. She had a wonderful smile on her face and tears on her cheeks. She gave Iona a hug, and then my mother and father as well.

The next day she arrived on time in the office with the joy of the Lord all over her face! She wasn't swearing, cursing, or losing her temper! The other workers started asking her questions. "What happened to you?" "Have you got religion?" "Are you a Baptist now like Iona?"

She said, "What happened to me was that I gave my heart to Jesus Christ, and He forgave me of all my sins! I am filled with His peace and joy!"

She was a new creation. Her work was excellent, efficient, and on time! Her bosses were amazed and deeply touched by her story, and they took the time to sit down with Iona to hear a personal account of her conversion!

She was healed from her old nature, by the "Touch of the Master's Hand!"

Chapter Three

PERSONAL PERMEATION

INTRODUCTION

The Oxford dictionary gives three definitions for the word *saint*.

- A very good or holy person whom Christians believe will go to heaven after they die.
- A very good or holy person who is officially declared to be a saint by the Christian church after they die.
- Informal: a very kind or patient person.[16]

The false teaching of the Roman Catholic Church has influenced people for centuries, and this includes the Protestants as well. In fact, that also means the Oxford dictionary!

Here are the false teachings of the Roman Catholic Church for your consideration:[17]

---

[16] *Compact Oxford English Dictionary of Current English* (Oxford University Press), 909.

[17] The information provided above is supported in material produced by the United States Conference of Catholic Bishops, under the title of "Saints."

- Sainthood cannot be claimed until the candidate has been dead and buried for five years.
- At the appropriate fifth anniversary of the candidate's death, the following steps can begin:
  o The "Servant of God" status is granted by the pope, meaning that the candidate is qualified for consideration.
  o "Venerable" is the title given to the Servant of God based on the life of heroic virtue and because the candidate has worked aggressively to improve himself or herself spiritually.
  o "Blessed" is declared after the first miracle attributed to the grave of the candidate. Pilgrims having traveled to that graveside and offered prayers to the "saint to be" left behind them canes, crutches, and or wheelchairs. This is referred to as "beatification."
  o Following the beatification of the candidate, a second miracle is required to move up to the canonization conducted by the pope.
  o He then declares "sainthood." The new saint can now answer prayers of the faithful.

Mariolatry declares that the Virgin Mary is "the Mother of God" and that she will hear and answer our prayers more reliable than her Son named Jesus! In fact, Mary is to be worshipped because the religious belief of the Roman Church declares that Mary was conceived without the sinful nature possessed by all human beings!

Mary would be the first to protest such a blasphemy as this claim that she was free from all sin!

Listen to Mary worshipping the Lord in her "Magnificat."

> And Mary said, "My soul magnifies the LORD, and my spirit has rejoiced in God my Savior ..." (Luke 1:46–47)

In the entire "Magnificat," Mary quoted twenty-three references in the Old Testament prophecies concerning the Baby Jesus and the grace that was granted to her so that she could be His earthly physical mother! Mary was never referred to as "the Mother of God" in either the Old Testament or the New Testament.

1 Timothy 2:5

> For there is one God, and one Mediator between God and men, the Man Christ Jesus!

Lorraine Boettner

> In the year 610 AD, Pope Boniface IV first suggested the celebration of All Saints Festival and ordered that the Pantheon, a pagan temple in Rome that had been dedicated to all the gods, should be converted to a Christian church, and the relics of the saints placed therein. He then dedicated the church to the Blessed Virgin Mary and all the martyrs. Thus the worship of Mary and the saints replaced the heathen gods and goddesses, and it was merely a case of one error being substituted for another.[18]

Isaiah 42:8

> I am the LORD, that is My Name; and My glory I will not give to another, nor My praise to carved images!

God's right to glory is nonnegotiable! He will not share that reverence and worship with any of His saints, with His ecclesiastical VIPs, or

---

[18] Lorraine Boettner, *Roman Catholicism* (London: The Banner of Truth), 130.

with the Virgin Mary who was chosen by God's grace to be the earthly mother of the Son of Man, Jesus! (Philippians 2:5–11)

Alexander Hislop

> The Babylonians, in their popular religion, supremely worshipped a goddess mother and a son, who was represented in pictures and images as an infant or child in his mother's arms. From Babylon this worship of the mother and the child spread to the ends of the earth. In Egypt, the mother and child were worshipped under the names of Isis and Osiris. In India, even to this day, as Isi and Iswara; in Asia, as Cybele and Deoius; in pagan Rome, as Fortuna and Jupiter-puer or Jupiter the boy; in Greece, as Ceres, the Great Mother, with the babe at her breast, or as Irene, the goddess of peace, with the boy Plutus in her arms; and even in Tibet, in China, and Japan, the Jesuit missionaries were astonished to find the counterpart of Madonna and her child as devoutly worshipped as in papal Rome itself.[19]

The Word of God emphatically condemns the concept of praying to Mary, to the pope, or to any of the saints who have been "dead for five years" and "beatified" by the council or the pope as human beings! All contacts with dead people are condemned in scripture (Deuteronomy 18:9–12; Exodus 22:18; Leviticus 20:6; Isaiah 8:19–20).

All saints and angels strongly refuse to be worshipped (Acts 10:25, 26 [Peter]; Acts 14:14–15 [Paul]; Revelation 22:8–9 [John]).

---

[19] Alexander Hislop, *The Two Babylons* (Moody Publishers), 27.

ACTS 1:4, 5, 8

> And being assembled together with them, He commanded them not to depart from Jerusalem, but to wait for the Promise of the Father, which, He said, you have heard from Me;
>
> For John truly baptized with water, but you shall be baptized with the Holy Spirit not many days from now ...
>
> But you shall receive power when the Holy Spirit has come upon you; and you shall be witnesses to Me in Jerusalem, and in all Judea and Samaria, and to the end of the earth.

Similarly, the word *apostolos* (apostle) was limited to the twelve men Jesus selected after a night of prayer. Only once was there a replacement for an apostle after his death, and he was Judas Iscariot, who committed suicide. No one, except Matthias, had the privilege of being chosen to join the apostles in those early days of the church.

There is no evidence of "apostolic succession" or of anyone chosen by Christ to speak on His behalf with divine authority! Our authority belongs to Jesus and provides us with supernatural ministry in every age and all over our world!

Later, the wonderful conversion and calling of Saul of Tarsus on the road to Damascus added him to the ministry of the apostles. It equipped him for evangelism, church planting, and writing thirteen New Testament books for believers through two thousand years!

What then did the apostle Paul call other believers? Were they "disciples" or "followers of Christ" as it is popular among pastors today?

Paul referred to male believers as brothers (133 times) and "sisters" for female believers. In the early days of the evangelization of the world, the believers were known as "People of the Way" (Acts 9:2; 19:9; 19:23; 22:4; 24:14, 22). The first time these believers in Jesus were called "Christians" occurred in Antioch (Acts 11:26; 26:28; 1 Peter 4:16).

ANOTHER WORD: AGAPE

The Greek language in the New Testament uses three words translated as "love."

a. *Storgos* means "a natural, gravitational love; an instinctive concern for one's offspring; found in both animals and man. Only the negative form, *astorgos,* is used in scripture (Romans 1:31).

b. *Philos* means a beautiful and friendly love. Paul describes this in Romans 12:10.

c. *Agapeo* means a divine love found only in God. (It is also found in born-again believers.)[20]

AGAPEO

The noun and verb form of this Greek word for divine love is found 320 times in the New Testament, with sixty-two in the four Gospels but nowhere in the book of Acts!

Agape was never found in any human being prior to the Day of Pentecost when the Holy Spirit took up eternal indwelling in the bodies of Christians (1 Corinthians 6:19–20; 2 Corinthians

---

[20] Dr. H. L. Willmington, *Willmington's Guide to the Bible* (Wheaton, Illinois: Tyndale House Publishers, Inc.), 451.

6:14–18). Furthermore, the usage of agape in the four Gospels was strictly for illustration and commandments for our fellowship with other believers. The disciples were "Old Testament" believers until they received the baptism of the Holy Spirit in the upper room, and they became New Testament children of God (John 1:6–13; 3:3–8).

BIBLICAL SAINTHOOD

The New Testament term is *hagios,* meaning "sanctified." This term is used sixty-seven times in the New Testament, including some observations below:

- Saints were chosen by God's grace before the world was created (Ephesians 1:4)!
- Sainthood is a gift of grace, not a reward for "holy" living (Ephesians 2:8–9).
- Sainthood is received at the new birth (John 1:10–13).
- Saints are also adopted into God's family (Romans 8:15–17).
- Sainthood is the power for us to live holy lives (2 Corinthians 5:17).
- Sainthood blends our old natures with our new natures (Romans 7:18–25).
- Sainthood occurs when the Holy Spirit sanctifies and seals us at conversion through faith in Jesus alone for salvation (Ephesians 1:11–14; 1 Corinthians 6:9–11)!
- Every saint was dead in trespasses and sin until their new birth (Ephesians 2:1–10)! But God loved us when we hated Him. He brought us to life when we were spiritually dead, because of His great agape love demonstrated in the crucifixion of His Only Begotten Son on the cross of Calvary. Through His infinite grace, God lifted us up from the miry clay, placed our feet upon the Rock, established

our goings, and put a new song in our mouths, even praise to our God, and He sat us in the heavenly places in Christ Jesus! Hallelujah!

Called by God to be a saint!

Sainthood belongs to every Christian.

Romans 1:7	To all who are in Rome, beloved of God, called to be saints.
1 Corinthians 1:2	To the church of God which is at Corinth, to those who are sanctified in Christ Jesus, called to be saints, with all who in every place call on the Name of Jesus Christ our Lord, both theirs and ours.
2 Corinthians 1:1	To the church of God which is in Corinth, with all the saints who are in Achaia ...
Ephesians 1:1	To the saints who are in Ephesus, and faithful in Christ Jesus ...
Philippians 1:1	To all the saints in Christ Jesus who are in Philippi, with the bishops (pastors) and deacons ...
Colossians 1:1	To the saints and faithful brethren in Christ who are in Colosse ...

Disciples Transferred to Saints

The frustration of the disciples rested in their inability to understand the teaching of Jesus (Matthew 13:36), their inability to deliver a son who was demonized (Matthew 17:14–21), their fear of dying in the boat that was enduring a storm (Mark 4:35–41), plus many other issues.

The disciples, including the seventy who were sent out on a visitation ministry, and the others who were gathered as a group of 120 who were locked into the upper room for fear of the Jews.

Some pastors have suggested that these disciples were attending a prayer meeting that resulted in the coming of the Holy Spirit! Such a claim is a case of eisegesis (reading your own view into the text of scripture) instead of exegesis (discovering what the Word of God is actually saying and submitting to His Word).

The 120 disciples in the upper room were filled with anxiety and fear. The coming of the Holy Spirit was on the divine schedule and for the purpose of bringing the church into spiritual existence and empowered for serving the King of kings in a lost world!

Now each disciple was free of struggling with his own willpower to live for Jesus, to the amazing miracle of having Jesus living within their own bodies!

Galatians 2:20

> I have been crucified with Christ; it is no longer I
> who live, but Christ lives in me; and the life which
> I now live in the flesh I live by faith in the Son of
> God, Who loved me and gave Himself for me.

When a lost sinner receives forgiveness through the salvation provided by Jesus Christ, he doesn't become a disciple; he becomes a saint!

One of my favorite devotional books, titled *Awake My Heart* by J. Sidlow Baxter, was first published in 1960. In the early material found in this book, Baxter writes,

> The meaning of the word "saint" is exactly the same as "sanctify." True sainthood is Christian sanctification or separatedness—separatedness from our unregenerate past, from worldliness, from all known sinful ways, and separatedness to an outward confession of Christ, and an inward fellowship with Christ, and a daily usefulness by Christ. The first business of every Christian is this sanctification or separatedness, and the development of holy character. This is not incompatible with legitimate employment in business, unless our occupation itself is wrong. We can make all our circumstances contribute, if we will, to the furtherance of real sainthood. This is the highest of all callings; and this is the supreme glory of the Christian life.[21]

Every saint has the following list of blessings provided by the indwelling Holy Spirit:

- Security
  Eternal security is the foundation of the Gospel of grace, offering everlasting life to souls that are dead in trespasses and sin!

---

[21] J. Sidlow Baxter, *Awake My Heart* (Grand Rapids, Michigan: Zondervan Publishing House), 22.

Note: John 3:14–21; 5:24; 10:27–30; 14:1–6; Romans 3:21–26; 5:1–5; 6:23; 8:1; 10:9–13

- Scripture
  The Word of God was inspired by the Holy Spirit so that every word in it has been divinely protected from error and deceit. The same Holy Spirit also illuminates our minds and souls as we study His inspired Word. In that way, the Bible moves us toward the Lord from our inner most being.

  Note: Hebrews 1:1–4; 2 Timothy 3:16–17; 2 Peter 1:18–21; 2 Corinthians 3:14–4:6

- Safety
  Spiritual warfare is mainly engaged between our ears! Our minds are the targets in satanic strategy, but the Lord has provided us with safety in such a battle!

  Note: 2 Corinthians 10:1–6; Romans 12:1–2; Ephesians 6:10–13 (We'll take a close look at this passage later.)

- Service
  Serving the Lord is allowing the Holy Spirit to produce His fruit that we will bear by His grace.

  Note: John 15:1–8, 16; Galatians 5:16, 22–26

- Supplies
  Our Lord is filled with grace that will provide us with what we need so that we can serve Him in all circumstances!

  Note: Matthew 6:25–34; Philippians 4:10–13, 19; Psalm 23:1–6

- Sanctification
  The Lord's purpose in salvation is that His children should demonstrate His holiness.

  Note: Romans 6:5–14; 8:28–29; 1 John 2:15–17; 1 Thessalonians 4:1–8; 1 Peter 1:13–16; Ephesians 4:17–32

- Soul Winning
  Leading lost souls to faith in Jesus Christ is the best experience any Christian can have after his or her own conversion!

  Note: Proverbs 11:30; Daniel 12:3; Acts 1:8; Matthew 9:35–38; John 4:35–38; Acts 18:9–10

In his excellent devotional material, Dr. Charles Stanley made the following remarks about the Day of Pentecost when the church was born:

> We don't need to pray specific words for the Spirit to arrive. Nor do we have to attend a special service invoking His presence in order for Him to dwell in us. Any teaching that claims that we can lose the Spirit and must regain Him over and over again is false.
>
> As soon as we trust in Jesus, His Spirit comes to abide with us forever (Jn. 14:16). This truth is essential to understand, because Scripture clearly says that anyone who doesn't have the Spirit does not belong to Christ (Ro. 8:9)
>
> It would be impossible to live the Christian life without the indwelling Spirit. He's the One who

guides us into God's will, teaches us the truths of Scripture, transforms us into Christ's likeness, and empowers us to serve and obey God successfully and joyfully.[22]

The "Biblical Boot Camp" will be introduced in chapters 4–6 as we describe "The Panoply of God," "The Power of God," and "The Privilege of Prayer."

---

[22] Dr. Charles Stanley, *In Touch Devotional, p.* 25.

THE MASTER'S TOUCH

He was a big and a muscular Ontario Provincial Police officer and had very little interest in his wife's faith in Jesus Christ! She did her best to bring her husband under the message of the Gospel. She was successful in bringing him to our church services on Sunday mornings. He would sit near the front with her and listened to every sermon carefully.

He expected to find the flaws in these messages that would prove that we were all hypocrites, and he could refuse to attend church with her! The trouble was that he could not find that inconsistency and could not deny that the Gospel was penetrating through his mind to his heart.

On one Sunday morning, I was sitting on the platform with our worship team and the Holy Spirit was already drawing him to the foot of the cross. The Spirit said to me, "This is his day! Don't let him leave without praying with him!"

After the sermon, I gave an altar call for those who would give their hearts to the Lord, but no one responded to the invitation. That was unusual because we had been blessed with watching the Spirit of God transforming sinners into saints!

After the benediction, I moved down from the platform and headed straight toward him. As I shook his hand, I said, "We are so glad that you have been coming to our morning services with your wife for quite a few weeks! Now this is your day! This is your time to find Jesus Christ as your Savior and Lord! Come with me to my study, and we'll talk about this experience."

Tim followed me without a protest or excuse, but with his head down and his eyes damp with tears.

In my office, I led him through the Gospel presentation and answered all of the questions he wanted to bring up. At the end, he chose to surrender to the Lord and prayed with me to become a child of the King! The angels were celebrating in heaven, and his wife was celebrating with her friends in the auditorium as we returned from my study!

Now his profession was blessed by the Lord and he was able to take training for the role of detective. That was then increased into the role of plainclothes and undercover detective working among the criminal underworld.

One day he phoned me and booked a personal meeting in my study. When we met, it was obvious that he was very troubled and worried. He said, "Pastor, I'm in a terrible conflict with my new faith in Jesus and the demands of my job!"

He went on to describe the sinful things he had to do so that he would be accepted by the underworld! He had to use filthy language, drink alcohol, smoke cigarettes, and flirt with the women in the bars and nightclubs! He said, "Pastor, what does the Lord think about this? Should I resign and move back to street cop in uniform?"

I asked him how his wife felt about it, and he assured me that she was the one who urged him to have this appointment with me. I said, "Human wisdom is very limited, and we need the direction that only the Spirit of the Living God could give! Let's talk to Jesus for a few minutes."

I led him in prayer, and then he also cried out to the Lord and asked Him to give him the clear direction God would bless.

Later he stopped me after the morning service and said, "Pastor, congratulate me! You are looking at a Christian constable who walks his beat with a clean conscience!"

Chapter Four

PREPARATION

("Biblical Boot Camp")

Photos below: preparing the soldiers for human warfare.

While military training has its demanding boot camp for the new men and women who have joined their forces, we who belong to Jesus Christ need to engage in discipline and preparation for spiritual warfare!

We need to understand what the "Captain of our Salvation" has provided for each of us so that we will be able to serve Him under all circumstances! This chapter will examine some of the principles that belong to the "Onward Christian Soldiers!"

Onward Christian Soldiers

Onward Christian Soldiers, marching as to war,
With the cross of Jesus going on before.
Christ, the Royal Master, leads against the foe;
Forward into battle see His banners go! ...
Like a mighty army moves the Church of God;
Brothers (sisters) we are treading where the saints
have trod.
We are not divided, all one body we,
One in hope and doctrine, one in charity (agape).[23]

THE ENLISTMENT PRINCIPLE (2 TIMOTHY 2:1–4)

Every believer has been conscripted by the Captain of our Salvation, and we are all engaged in spiritual warfare! No one has the right to opt out or to commit the crime of AWOL!

2 Timothy 2:1–4

You, therefore my son, be strong in the grace that is in Christ Jesus

And the things that you have heard from me among many witnesses, commit these to faithful men who will be able to teach others also.

---

[23] Sabine Baring-Gould (1834–1924).

You therefore must endure hardship as a good soldier of Jesus Christ.

No one engaged in warfare entangles himself with the affairs of this life, that he may please him who enlisted him as a soldier.

1 Timothy 1:18

This charge I commit to you, son Timothy, according to the prophecies previously made concerning you, that by them you may wage the good warfare.

1 Timothy 6:12

Fight the good fight, lay hold on eternal life, to which you were called and have confessed the good confession in the presence of many witnesses.

THE ENABLING PRINCIPLE (EPHESIANS 6:10–11)

Finally, my brethren, be strong in the Lord and in the power of His might.

Put on the whole armor of God, that you may be able to stand against the wiles of the devil.

GRAMMAR LESSONS

The word translated as "Be strong" is *endunamousthe*, which is in the present tense, passive voice, and imperative mood. That tells us that this action is continuous (present tense), is yielding to the strength of the Lord (passive), and (imperative) is not a divine suggestion! It is an order from our Chief Commander in His own spiritual army!

Just compare with Ephesians 5:18 ("Be filled") *(playrousthe)*, present passive imperative equals "keep on being filled with the Holy Spirit!"; strong/power/might.

Allow yourself to be strengthened continuously in the power: *kratei* means "His infinite strength," and *ischus* means "His infinite might!"

This amazing verse introduces us to the "biblical boot camp" and to the divine plan for our protection and victory in spiritual warfare!

Ephesians 6:10 says,

> Finally, brethren, keep on being strengthened in the
> Lord and in the power of His might!

OBSERVATIONS

You are required to continue surrendering yourself to the infinite and omnipotent strength of our Lord!

He is the Creator, Sustainer, Savior, and the Captain of our Salvation!

His strength stands available for each and every believer and is received when you request it in genuine faith!

This commandment is grammatically identical with Ephesians 5:18.

> And do not be drunk with wine, in which is
> dissipation; but continually be filled with the Holy
> Spirit.

POWER!

The apostle Paul made a statement concerning God's power in his letter to the church in Rome! He said,

> For I am not ashamed of the gospel of Christ, for it is the power (dunamis) of God to salvation for everyone who believes, for the Jew first (historically) and also for the Greek (Gentiles).

> For in it the righteousness of God is revealed from faith to faith; as it is written, "The just shall live by faith." (Romans 1:16–17; Paul was quoting Habakkuk 2:4.)

The word *dunamis* carries within itself a number of meanings. We will only mention the following two:

- "inherent power, power residing in a thing by virtue of its nature, or which a person or thing exerts and puts forth"[24] In other words, Jesus possessed dunamis because He was, is, and shall forever be the Second Person of the Triunity, the Anointed One by God the Father as the Messiah of Israel, the Savior of all believers, and the King of kings and Lord of Lords who will reign on the throne of His earthly father named David.

- "specifically, the power of performing miracles"[25] Jesus was born miraculously through a young virgin named Mary. She was not chosen by God because she was previously born without original sin, as found in every human being in our race! In fact, Mary worshipped her God of grace for

---

[24] Joseph Henry Thayer, *Greek-English Lexicon of the New Testament* (Grand Rapids, Michigan: Zondervan Publishing House), 159.
[25] Ibid., 159.

sending her Savior into our world! (See Mary's "Magnificat" in Luke 1:46–56.)

The power of Jesus was passed on to all of those who were born again by the indwelling Spirit and who were declared to be the children of the omnipotent Lord Jesus Christ!

See Acts 1:8.

> But you shall receive power (dunamis) when the Holy Spirit has come upon you; and you shall be witnesses to Me in Jerusalem, and in all of Judea, and Samaria, and to the end of the earth.

ETYMOLOGY

The New Testament Greek word *dunamis* is the root for a series of English words.

Dynamite means "an explosive compound of nitroglycerin held in some absorbent substance."

Dynamo means "a generator for the conversion of mechanical energy into electrical power."

Dynamic means "a person characterized by energy or forcefulness."

THE POWER OF GOD

Omnipotence

God can do anything that can be done if it does not contradict His holy nature.

- He cannot create a rock too heavy for Him to lift.
- He cannot so something that would involve Him in sin.
- God has all sovereign power and authority over nature, humanity, life and death, angels, demons (fallen angels), Satan (the originator or "the Luciferian Rebellion" in which one-third of the angels joined in his wretched mutiny against the God of creation, Providence, and grace!) See Revelation 12:4.

The apostle Paul was determined that the believers in Ephesus would have a clear understanding of the Lord and Savior, Jesus Christ.

Ephesians 1:15–23

> Therefore I also, after I heard of your faith in the Lord Jesus and your love for all the saints,
>
> Do not cease to give thanks for you, making mention of you in my prayers;
>
> That the God of our Lord Jesus Christ, may give you the spirit of wisdom and revelation in the knowledge of Him,
>
> The eyes of your understanding being enlightened; that you may know what is the hope of His calling, what are the riches of the glory of His inheritance in the saints.

Ephesians 3:14–21

> For this reason I bow my knees to the Father of our Lord Jesus Christ, from whom the whole family in heaven and earth is named, that He would grant you, according to the riches of His glory, to be

strengthened with might through His Spirit in the inner man, that Christ may dwell in your hearts through faith; that you, being rooted and grounded in love, may be able to comprehend with all the saints what is the width and length and depth and height—

to know the love of Christ which passes knowledge; that you may be filled with all the fullness of God.

Now to Him who is able to do exceedingly abundantly above all that we ask or think, according to the power that works in us, to Him be glory in the church by Christ Jesus to all generations forever and ever. Amen.

THE EQUIPPING PRINCIPLE (EPHESIANS 6:11–13)

Put on the whole armor of God that you may be able to stand against the wiles (schemings) of the devil.

For we do not wrestle against flesh and blood, but against principalities, against powers, against the rulers of the darkness of this age, against spiritual hosts of wickedness in the heavenly places,

Therefore, take up the whole armor of God, that you may be able to withstand in the evil day, and having done all, to stand.

One of my favorite books for Christians, and especially for pastors, is titled *Why Revival Tarries,* by Leonard Ravenhill. In chapter 6, he writes,

The only power that God yields to is that of prayer. We will write about prayer-power, but not fight while in prayer. A title, undeniably true of the Church today, would be **"We Wrestle Not!"** We will display our gifts, natural or spiritual; we will air our views, political or spiritual; we will preach a sermon or write a book to correct a brother in doctrine. But who will storm hell's stronghold? Who will say the devil <u>nay</u>? Who will deny himself good food or good company or good rest that hell may gaze upon him wrestling, embarrassing demons, liberating captives, depopulating hell, and leaving, in answer to his travail, a stream of blood-washed souls?[26]

We are commanded to "put on the whole armor of God" for use in spiritual warfare. However, this clear commandment needs to be correctly expounded so that we would experience miraculous victory in our battles!

GRAMMAR STUDY

"Put on" is not a continuing procedure as we face each morning!

The Greek word is endusasthe, which is in aorist, middle, and imperative.

This formula is frequently used for a strong reason. We are not to put the armor of God on every morning and hang them up in our closet at night! The armor is given to us at the moment of our conversion by faith in Jesus Christ alone for salvation!

The use of aorist indicates that the action is a point in time, not a process. The same format is used by Paul in Romans 13:14.

---

[26] Leonard Ravenhill, *Why Revival Tarries* (Bethany House Publishers), 60.

But <u>put on</u> the Lord Jesus Christ, and make no provision for the flesh to fulfill its lusts.

The "middle" voice indicates that the action is performed by both the Lord and the believer at the same time.

The imperative mood is not a divine suggestion but a clear commandment that the Lord wants each of us to obey!

"The whole armor" indicates that we are not allowed to pick out a special piece of armor provided by the Lord! God has given us everything we could ever need in the struggles of our lives!

The armor is His, provided to us by His wonderful grace! The armor of God is not made of metal or leather but is spiritual and filled with the Spirit's omnipotence!

The spiritual armor provides a character and spiritual strength to protect us from satanic schemes on the one hand and to equip us for fruitfulness in His service.

SIMILAR USAGES

- Romans 13:14 (as mentioned above)

- Galatians 3:27
  For as many of you as were baptised into Christ (spiritual, not water baptism, which takes place at your conversion. (cf. Romans 6:3–6)

- Colossians 3:14
  But above all these things <u>put on love</u> (agape), which is the bond of perfection."

- Matthew 28:19

  Go therefore and <u>make disciples of all the nations</u>, baptizing them in the Name of the Father and of the Son and of the Holy Spirit ...

"Make disciples ..." is in the same structure as discussed above: the aorist, middle, imperative (a point of action completed, and not a progressive process).

Adrenalin: "a hormone produced by the adrenal glands that increases rates of blood circulation, breathing, and carbohydrate metabolism."[27]

Adrenalin is a gracious system placed into humanity at the time of creation in the Garden of Eden. Its surge of energy and strength enable the man or woman to either flee or fight (or both!)

At the spiritual birth, each sinner received the indwelling Holy Spirit who provides the saint with God's power to either flee or fight or both!

1 Timothy 6:11, 12

> But you, O man of God, <u>flee these things</u> and pursue righteousness, godliness, faith, love, patience, gentleness.

> <u>Fight the good fight of faith</u>, lay hold on eternal life, to which you were also called and have confessed the good confession in the presence of many witnesses.

---

[27] *Compact Oxford English Dictionary* (Oxford University Press), 12.

THE MASTER'S TOUCH

On a Friday afternoon, I was busy setting up chairs for a staff prayer/praise meeting the next day. We were sharing the gospel at the Leamington District Agricultural Fair in the arena.

In five days, we had led 205 people to a profession of faith in Jesus Christ! Among those many souls were two prostitutes, a drug dealer, a criminal gang leader, an alcoholic, and a daredevil stunt driver.

One of our young men came into the room accompanied by the foreman of the Hell Drivers who would be performing on Saturday afternoon. "Natch" (his nickname) was all muscle and toughness poured into a tight T-shirt and blue jeans.

Our conversation was brief and to the point! I heard myself saying to him, "Natch, you're only half a man! You are strong and skilled in physical things, but you have no relationship with the Lord God to whom you must give an account when your life on earth is done! In fact, a Christian can do what you do and a lot better! Why? Because a child of the Lord has His presence with them every moment of every day!"

Then Natch said, "OK, Preacher! You're on!"

I said, "What do you mean by that?"

He said, "Two o'clock tomorrow afternoon, you will ride with me! Be in the infield no later than 1:45!"

That afternoon I rode with Natch and his boss as they drove their cars at seventy-five miles per hour over jumps in the middle of the dirt track and then did power circles, crisscrossing each other. They then set up for a second run over the jumps.

As we sat in his car, Natch said, "You've done this before, haven't you?"

I said, "I have not ever ridden in such a car before, and certainly not over jumps at seventy-five miles per hour!"

Natch replied, "Well, why weren't you scared?"

I said, "Because you were not the driver! Over forty of my people have been praying for us since yesterday afternoon! I knew that Jesus was in charge of you and of this car, so there was no reason to be afraid!"

This friendship went on for months before Natch surrendered his life to the Lord Jesus Christ and eventually became a "Heaven Driver" instead of a "Hell Driver"!

His drunkenness, fighting, cursing, gambling, and womanizing came to a stop, and the new man found it impossible to keep on the lifestyle associated with his role on the Hell Drivers stunt team!

He resigned and settled his life as a testimony of what Jesus can do with a lost soul through His gift of grace.

Chapter Five

THE PANOPLY

Our English word used in this title comes from the original Greek word in Ephesians 6:11 that says, "Put on the <u>whole armor</u> of God, that you may be able to stand against the wiles (schemes) of the devil."

The word is *panoplia,* meaning "full armor, complete armor."[28]

The grammatical issue evident in this verse has been discussed previously (part 2's chapter 4).

The main concept in this grammatical structure is that we are commanded to put on the armor of God once and forever! It is an aorist, middle, imperative verbal usage that is for point action rather than progressive action.

Therefore, we saints don't take the armor provided by our Heavenly Father so that we can hang them up in the closet while we sleep! We don't get up in the morning and select the pieces of armor that we will probably need during the day before us!

---

[28] Fritz Rienecker and Cleon Rogers, *Linguistic Key to the Greek New Testament* (Grand Rapids, Michigan: The Zondervan Corporation), 541.

The armor of God is a *gift of His grace received in the instant that we are born again through faith in Jesus alone for eternal life!*

THE LISTED ARMOR OF GOD

1. Girdle/Belt

"This belt held other weapons within easy reach for the soldier." The girdle varied from two to six inches in width, made of leather, and sometimes studded with iron, silver, or gold.

Often the girdle was supported by a shoulder strap, and it could carry a scrip, a sword, or other weapons.

The belt that provided access to the weapons was symbolic of integrity, honesty, and truthfulness!

"Stand therefore, <u>having girded your waist with truth</u>" (Ephesians 6:14).

Truthfulness is the essential foundation of our effective Christian witness! The number 1 excuse for people not attending church services: "I don't go to church because of all the hypocrites there!"

2. Breastplate

"The breastplate was essential because it protected the heart and vital organs …"

The breastplate is used in this passage of scripture as a symbol of our personal and practical righteousness. There are two types of righteousness in our redemption. Imputed righteousness is the gift of God's grace, who gives us the perfect righteousness of His

Son, Jesus, when He pays the price for our forgiveness (Ephesians 2:8–10; Romans 3:21–26). Imparted righteousness is the gift of God's grace through the ministry of the Holy Spirit leading us in a close walk with the Lord (Galatians 2:20; 5:16; 5:22–23; Ephesians 5:14–21).

3. The Helmet

The *perikephalaia* was the Greek version of the Hebrew word *kobha*. The materials of the helmet were, at first, wood, linen, felt, or even rushes; leather was used until it was supplanted by bronze.

The helmet was designed to protect the brain and is of extreme importance. The brain is not only the center of our thinking; it also provides the bodily motor functions and automatic physiological response to stimuli.

The thought life of a Christian is the key to his or her spiritual maturity and the transformation of our lives!

Most spiritual warfare is waged between the ears! Satan knows that if he could control our thinking, then he can control out behavior!

Proverbs 23:7

> For as he thinks in his heart, so is he.

Romans 12:1, 2

> I beseech you therefore, brethren, by the mercies of God, that you present your bodies a living sacrifice, holy, acceptable to God, which is your reasonable service.

And do not be conformed to this world, but be transformed by the renewing of your mind, that you may prove what is that good and acceptable and perfect will of God.

2 Corinthians 10:3–6

For though we walk in the flesh, we do not war according to the flesh.

For the weapons of our warfare are nor carnal but mighty in God for pulling down strongholds,

Casting down arguments and every high thing that exalts itself against the knowledge of God, bringing every thought into captivity to the obedience of Christ,

And being ready to punish all disobedience when your obedience is fulfilled.

Ephesians 4:17–32

This I say, therefore, and testify in the Lord, that you should no longer walk as the rest of the Gentiles walk, in the futility of their mind,

Having their understanding darkened, being alienated from the life of God, because of the ignorance that is in them, because of the blindness of their heart;

Who, being past feeling, have given themselves over to lewdness, to work all uncleanness with greediness.

But you have not so learned Christ,

If indeed you have heard Him and have been taught by Him, as the truth is in Jesus:

That you put off, concerning your former conduct, the old man which grows corrupt according to the deceitful lusts,

And be renewed in the spirit of,

And that you put on the new man which was created according to God, in true righteousness and holiness.

4. The Sword

"And <u>take</u> the helmet of salvation, and the sword of the Spirit, which is the Word of God" (Ephesians 6:17).

The word "take" that I have underlined above is a different Greek word from the command to "put on" that occurs at salvation.

The word for the believer to use the armor of God (Ephesians 6:13): "Therefore <u>take up the whole armor of God</u> ...") The word is *analambano* used in the aorist, active, imperative and means the following:

> The word was used as a military technical term describing the last preparation and final step necessary before the actual battle begins.[29]

---

[29] Fritz Rienecker, *Linguistic Key to the Greek New Testament* (Grand Rapids, Michigan: The Zondervan Corporation), 541.

The implication here is that every soldier of the King of kings has been equipped with God's "panoply" of spiritual armor as a gift of redemption. Thereafter, we are commanded to take up all of the armor as a step of preparation for spiritual warfare!

The Word of God is described as a sword in Hebrews 4:12–13.

> For the Word of God is living and powerful, and sharper than any two-edged sword, piercing even to the division of soul and spirit, and of joints and marrow, and is a discerner of the thoughts and intents of the heart.
>
> "And there is no creature hidden from His sight, but all things are naked and open to the eyes of Him to Whom we must give account.

OTHER IMAGES

The Word of God is

- "a devouring flame" (Jeremiah 5:14)
- "a crushing hammer" (Jeremiah 23:29)
- "a guiding light" (Psalm 119:105, 130)
- "a purifying force" (John 15:3; 17:17)
- "food for the soul" (Psalm 119:103; 1 Peter 2:2)

THE AUTHORITY OF SCRIPTURE

Some "Christian" denominations base their faith on traditions and declarations made by the pope, archbishop, or the head of the religious body nationally or worldwide.

The Protestant Reformation was based on the following five *solae:*

1. sola scriptura ("by scripture alone")
2. sola fide ("by faith alone")
3. sola gratia ("by grace alone")
4. solus Christus ("Christ alone")
5. soli Deo gloria ("glory to God alone")

Our faith is based on the authority and inspiration of the Word of God (sixty-six books found in the Old Testament and New Testament of the Bible). The "Original Autographs" (the initial books of the Bible in the original languages) are inspired, inerrant, and infallible.

Inspiration: The text of scripture was "God-breathed" in such a way that the human authors maintained their style but wrote the text that was and is the Word of God and our authority for faith, Christian values, the message of the Gospel of Christ, and the standards for our lives.

Inerrant: The text that was written was protected by the Holy Spirit so that the Word of God was free of any and all errors.

Infallible: The text of the original autographs was never wrong about anything!

2 Timothy 3:16, 17

> All scripture is given by inspiration of God (theopneustos means "God-breathed"), and is profitable for doctrine, for reproof, for correction, for instruction in righteousness,
>
> That the man of God may be complete, thoroughly equipped for every good work.

2 Peter 1:20, 21

> Knowing this first, that no prophecy of Scripture is of any private interpretation,
>
> For prophecy never came by the will of man, but holy men of God spoke as they were moved by the Holy Spirit.

5. *Calligae*

Roman combat boots similar to our golf shoes!

> I used to love my FootJoys! They were comfortable and provided me with a firm stance for every shot on the golf course!
>
> The calligae were included in this list by Paul as an illustration of being prepared for sharing the Gospel in any situation! Every Christian needs to prepare their minds with a clear and convincing Gospel presentation!

Ephesians 6:15

> And having shod your feet with the preparation of the gospel of peace.

6. Shield of Faith

Ephesians 6:16

> Above all, taking the shield of faith (Scutum: a large door-shaped shield made with metal and coated

with wood soaked in water") <u>with which you will be able to quench all the fiery darts of the wicked one.</u>

The reference here to "faith" is not as in the body of our beliefs (as in Ephesians 4:13 and Jude 3), but this usage of faith is referring to our subjective faith in Jesus Christ day by day! Every satanic attack against you can be quenched and extinguished by the personal shield of faith!

Galatians 5:16

> I say then: walk in the Spirit, and you shall not fulfill the lust of the flesh.

1 John 4:4; 5:4

> He who is in you is greater than he who is in the world.
>
> For whatever is born of God overcomes the world. And this is the victory that has overcome the world—<u>our faith!</u>

THE PANOPLY OF GOD APPLIED

The armor of God is spiritual, not physical or material. We need to understand that our Savior is the Champion of Love who has never lost a battle since the foundation of the world!

The girdle/belt means integrity, honesty, and truthfulness.

The children of God are expected to behave in a manner that will be honest and truthful. The tragedy of today's evangelical church is that many believers stretch the truth or pretend to be what is not truthful at all!

Notice Paul's instructions to the believers in Ephesus.

> Therefore, putting away lying, "Let each one of you speak truth with his neighbor, for we are members of one another." (Ephesians 4:25)

Jesus taught the following to His disciples:

> But let your "Yes" be "Yes", and your "No" "No". For whatever is more than these is from the evil one." (Matthew 5:37)

The breastplate means imputed righteousness and imparted righteousness.

The breastplate was designed to protect the heart and the lungs of the soldier. The Lord has provided us with His "breastplate" at the moment of our conversion when we put our trust in Jesus alone for eternal life.

There are two kinds of righteousness in scripture for the children of God, and both are gifts of the grace of God. Self-righteousness is farce and the gate and broad way that leads to eternal suffering in hell!

> Enter by the narrow gate; for wide is the gate and broad is the way that leads to destruction, and there are many that go in by it.

> Because narrow is the gate and difficult is the way which leads to life, and there are few who find it. (Matthew 7:13, 14)

The Imputed Righteousness

Eternal life is only available to those who are free from all sin and guilt! That rules out every human being on planet Earth! However, God understood this tragic reality, and the Father, Son, and Holy Spirit provided a plan of redemption in which all sins could be forgiven, but all guilt would receive punishment as well!

Ephesians 1:3–9

Blessed be the God and Father of our Lord Jesus Christ, who has blessed us with every spiritual blessing in the heavenly places in Christ;

Just as He chose us in Him before the foundation of the world, that we should be holy and without blame before Him in love,

Having predestinated us to adoption as sons by Jesus Christ to Himself, according to the good pleasure of His will,

To the praise of the glory of His grace, by which He made us accepted in the Beloved.

In Him we have redemption through His blood, the forgiveness of sins, according to the riches of His grace

Which He made to abound before us in all wisdom and prudence,

Having made known to us the mystery of His will, according to His good pleasure which He purposed in Himself.

Jesus is described in Revelation 13:8 as "the Lamb slain from the foundation of the world." The Lord Jesus Christ was in perfect agreement with the Father and the Holy Spirit in describing the sacrifice of an innocent substitute who would take the guilt and punishment that belonged to those who would be redeemed! The Lamb of God would permit humankind to crucify Him in between two guilty criminals. One of those two received God's forgiveness and the promise from Jesus that he would be with Him in paradise that very day!

THE IMPARTED RIGHTEOUSNESS

The helmet means spiritual control over your mind.

The Holy Spirit indwells each believer for the purpose of having control over our thinking and decisions. Read what God's Word has to say about our minds.

For as he thinks in his heart, so is he. (Proverbs 23:7)

For out of the heart proceed evil thoughts, murders, adulteries, fornications, thefts, false witness, blasphemies.

These are the things which defile a man, but to eat with unwashed hands does not defile a man. (Matthew 15:19–20)

Gary R. Collins has written about thirty books on psychology and counseling and has been a professor of psychology at Trinity Evangelical Divinity School in Deerfield, Illinois. In his book titled *The Magnificent Mind,* he made the following observation:

> Consider, for example, the fact that no one knows what the mind is. It has tremendous power, but it cannot be seen, felt, weighed, or surgically dissected ... According to the Bible it can be Christlike or evil; it is able to be molded and manipulated, and it can give rise to the genius of Einstein, the creative of Beethoven, or the barbaric brutality of a Hitler.
>
> The mind influences how each of us lives and thinks. There is clear evidence the mind can be controlled—by others—twisted by distorted thinking, and molded by God.[30]

Romans 12:1, 2

> I beseech you therefore, brethren, by the mercies of God, that you present your bodies a living sacrifice, holy, acceptable to God, which is your reasonable service.
>
> And do not be conformed to this world, but be transformed by the renewing of your mind, that you may prove what is that good and acceptable and perfect will of God.

---

[30] Gary R. Collins, *The Magnificent Mind* (Waco, Texas: Word Books Publisher), 15.

2 Corinthians 10:4–5

> For the weapons of our warfare are not carnal but
> mighty in God for pulling down strongholds,

> Casting down arguments and every high thing that
> exalts itself against the knowledge of God, bringing
> every thought into captivity to the obedience of Christ.

The sword means the inspired Word of God.

The Bible consists of sixty-six books in the Old Testament and New Testament (thirty-nine in the Old Testament and twenty-seven in the New Testament). These books have been Spirit breathed through human writers, allowing no errors, contradictions, or false teaching. It is described this way in 2 Timothy 3:16.

> All Scripture is given by inspiration of God, and is
> profitable for doctrine, for reproof, for correction,
> for instruction in righteousness,

> That the man of God may be complete, thoroughly
> equipped for every good work.

Calligae means "Gospel shoes" (understanding shoes)!

These spiked shoes represent an adequate training in presenting the Gospel of Christ to lost souls. There is a vast difference between witnessing and winning lost souls with the Gospel! (My own experience transformed my entire life and ministry! I was introduced to Evangelism Explosion in November 1967 in Windsor at Riverside Baptist Church. This was the first international training conference.)

"EE," as we call it, presents the Gospel clearly and logically and releases the evangelist from anxiety and the interfering of fear!

Proverbs 29:25 says, "The fear of man brings a snare, but whoever trusts in the Lord shall be safe."

Shield of faith means trusting in Jesus and His Word.

The "faith" referred to in this shield is not our statement of faith, nor the lessons of our catechisms! This usage of the word "faith" is our personal trust in Jesus Christ for salvation, sanctification, service, and security from satanic attacks and his wiles!

This faith in the Lord will snuff out the fiery darts of the wicked one!

THEOLOGICAL TERMS

Justification

Justification is a legal term that describes our freedom from any and all future punishment for our guilt in sin. We have been declared "righteous" based on the imputing of the righteousness of Jesus to each and every child of the King!

Romans 8:1; John 5:24; Romans 5:1–11

Dr. Augustus H. Strong wrote,

> By justification we mean the judicial act of God by which, on account of Christ, to whom the sinner is united by faith, He declares that sinner to be no longer exposed to the penalty of the law, but to be restored to His favor.[31]

---

[31] Augustus H. Strong, *Systematic Theology* (Philadelphia: the Judson Press, 1907), 849.

Redemption

Dr. H. L. Wilmington provides three meanings for the word *redemption*.

1. "To pay a ransom price for something or someone."

Hebrews 9:12

> Not with the blood of goats and calves, but with His own blood He entered the Most Holy Place once for all, having obtained eternal redemption.

2. "To remove from a slave marketplace."

Galatians 3:13

> Christ has redeemed us from the curse of the law, having become a curse for us (for it is written, "Cursed is everyone who hangs on a tree."

3. "To effect a full release."

Romans 8:22, 23

> For we know that the whole creation groans and labors with birth pangs together until now.

> Not only that, but we also who have the first fruits of the Spirit, even we ourselves, eagerly waiting for the adoption, the redemption of our body.[32]

---

[32] Dr. H. L. Wilmington, *Wilmington's Guide to the Bible* (Wheaton, Illinois: Tyndale House Publishers, Inc.), 733.

Reconciliation

The Old Testament uses a Hebrew word *(kaphar)* that means "to cover something." The word is found eighty-three times: seventy-six times to describe "atonement" and seven times for "reconciliation."

The New Testament uses a Greek word *(allasso)* meaning to change from enmity to that of friendship.

One of the New Testament chapters makes a clear explanation of what reconciliation between God and sinners who are actually the enemies of their Creator! Before we look into the chapter I've just mentioned, consider these verses:

Ephesians 2:1–3

> And you He made alive, who were dead in trespasses and sins,
>
> In which you once walked according to the course of this world, according to the prince of the power of the air, the spirit who now works in the sons of disobedience,
>
> Among whom we all once conducted ourselves in the lusts of our flesh, fulfilling the desires of the flesh and of the mind, and were by nature children of wrath, just as the others.

Colossians 1:21

> And you, who once were alienated and enemies in your mind by wicked works, yet now He has reconciled …

And now we will consider the chapter mentioned at the beginning of this subject.

2 Corinthians 5:17–21

> Therefore, if anyone is in Christ, he is a new creation; old things have passed away; behold all things have become new.
>
> Now all things are of God, who has reconciled us to Himself through Jesus Christ, and has given us the ministry of reconciliation,
>
> That is, that God was in Christ reconciling the world to Himself, not imputing their trespasses to them, and has committed to us the word of reconciliation.
>
> Now then, we are ambassadors for Christ, as though God were pleading through us: we implore you on Christ's behalf, be reconciled to God.
>
> For He made Him who knew no sin to be sin for us, that we might become the righteousness of God in Him.

There are three major subjects presented by Paul to the believers in Corinth.

1. THE MIRACLE OF RECONCILIATION (5:17)

The *miracle of reconciliation* is experienced by people dead in their sins being brought to spiritual life through the Gospel of Jesus! The apostle Paul wrote these words to the church in Rome:

For I am not ashamed of the gospel of Christ, for it
is the power of God to salvation for everyone who
believes, for the Jew first and also for the Greek.
(Romans 1:16)

2. THE MINISTRY OF RECONCILIATION (5:18–20)

The second miracle of reconciliation in this passage is described in
2 Corinthians 5:18–20 and is assigned to each and every born-again
child of God! Sharing the Gospel could have been committed to the
myriad of angels who serve the Lord twenty-four/seven, but the Lord
chose the lost sinners who had been redeemed through the blood
shed by Jesus on the old rugged cross.

Note the clarity of the Word of God.

> Now all things are of God, who has reconciled us
> to Himself through Jesus Christ, and has given to
> us the ministry of reconciliation,
>
> That is, that God was in Christ reconciling the
> world to Himself, not imputing their trespasses
> to them, and has committed to us the word of
> reconciliation!
>
> Now then, we are ambassadors for Christ, as though
> God were pleading through us: we implore you
> on Christ's behalf, be reconciled to God in Him
> [emphasis mine].

Just as we observed that Christian soldiers are not volunteers but
were enlisted by Christ at the moment of conversion, now we are
challenged with the ministry of evangelism! It is not a service

dedicated to the special gifted people or to those who find it easy to speak to strangers and to clearly explain the Gospel of Jesus Christ! This ministry belongs to every saint!

3. THE MESSAGE OF RECONCILIATION (5:21)

The message of reconciliation is crystal clear in verse 21. The righteous Son of God sacrificed Himself to pay the penalty of our sins, and to provide a glorious home in heaven for evermore!

> For He made Him who knew no sin to be sin for
> us, that we might become the righteousness of God
> in Him.

God the Father offered His holy Son as an innocent substitute to receive the punishment that we deserve.

Jesus Christ died on the cross to pay the penalty of our sins, and He bore *our guilt* so that the children of God can become godly and Christlike in our live on earth.

When we are received into heaven, it will be on one basis entirely. *"Is your name written in the Lamb's Book of Life?"*

Revelation 21:27

> But there shall by no means enter into it (heaven)
> anything that defiles, or causes an abomination or
> a lie, but only those who are written in the Lamb's
> Book of Life.

2 Corinthians 6:2

> For He says: "In an acceptable time I have heard
> you, and in the day of salvation I have helped you".

> Behold now is the accepted time; behold, now is the
> day of salvation.

Chapter Six

THE POWER OF PRAYER

THE MASTER'S TOUCH

He was a religious leader in Israel, an expert in the Old Testament, born a Hebrew, a Pharisee of the Pharisees, and a zealot in protecting Judaism from the inroads of a new "religion" worshipping Jesus Christ! He was the young man approving of the stoning to death of the deacon named Stephen, and he took care of the coats of those who wanted to throw the stones.

Saul of Tarsus was given official authority from the Sanhedrin Council to arrest, imprison, torture, and eventually condemn to crucifixion or other brutal death!

On the road to Damascus with a team of officials, Saul was suddenly stopped in his tracks! A light that was supernatural and brighter than the noonday sun struck Saul down and committed him to blindness as he lay on the dusty road.

A voice spoke to him, saying, "Saul, Saul, why are you persecuting Me?" Saul replied, "Who are You, Lord?" Then the Lord said, "I am Jesus, whom you are persecuting. It is hard for you to kick against the goads!"

Saul was then helped on his way to Damascus, where he stayed in blindness for three days, somewhat reflecting the three days and nights that Jesus spent in a borrowed tomb!

After his conversion, Saul changed his name to Paul and was appointed by Jesus as one of His apostles. He became a powerful evangelist and missionary reaching huge crowds of Gentiles and establishing many churches.

As well as this productive ministry, Paul wrote thirteen of the New Testament epistles, even some of them while he was held in a prison!

"The Master's Touch" in the heart of an enemy of the Gospel illustrated the power of prayer! Just notice how the Holy Spirit caused the early church of Jesus Christ to grow and win multitudes of lost souls, in spite of the persecution that they faced under the Roman dynasty.

Peter preached the gospel in Jerusalem on the Day of Pentecost.

Acts 2:41   Then those who gladly received his word were baptized; and that day about <u>3,000 souls were added to them</u>.

2:42   And the Lord <u>added to the church daily such as should be saved</u>.

3:1–4:3   Peter and John continued to preach the gospel in Jerusalem and were cast into prison. However, many of those who heard the Word believed; <u>and the number of the men came to be about 5,000</u>.

4:5–5:11	The church continued in unity and fellowship. And through the hands of the Apostles many signs and wonders were done among the people. And they were all with one accord in Solomon's Porch. [vs. 14] And believers were increasingly added to the Lord, multitudes of both men and women.
5:28, 42; 6:1	At night an angel of the Lord came to Peter and John and set them free from the prison, and they went into the temple and proclaimed the gospel of Jesus Christ! The officers of the Sanhedrin went to the Apostles and brought them back to the council without violence.
Vs. 28	And the high priest asked them, "Did we not strictly command you not to teach in this Name? And look, you have filled Jerusalem with your doctrine, and intend to bring this Man's blood on us!" But Peter and the other Apostles answered and said, "We ought to obey God rather than men!"
Vs. 42	And daily in the temple, and in every house, they did not cease teaching and preaching Jesus as the Christ.
6:1	Now in those days, when the number of disciples was multiplying …
6:7	Then the Word of God spread, and the number of disciples multiplied greatly in Jerusalem, and a great many of the priests were obedient to the faith.

Following the conversion, Paul, called to be an apostle, filled with the Holy Spirit, served the Lord as an evangelist, teacher, and author of scripture, and the blessing of the Lord filled the saints in the church.

Acts 9:31   Then the churches throughout all Judea, Galilee and Samaria had peace and were edified. And walking in the fear of the Lord and in the comfort of the Holy Spirit they were multiplied.

Acts 21:20   The Apostle Paul was blessed and encouraged by the reports brought to him from the saints in Jerusalem:

When he had greeted them, he told in detail those things which God had done among the Gentiles through his ministry.

And when they heard it, they glorified the Lord. And they said to him, "You see, brother, how many myriads of Jews there are who have believed, and they are all zealous for the law."

The power of prayer was demonstrated in the early church. Consider Acts 4:31–33.

> And when they had prayed, the place where they were assembled together was shaken; and they were all filled with the Holy Spirit, and they spoke the Word of God with boldness.

> Now the multitude of those who believed were of one heart and one soul; neither did anyone say that any of the things that he possessed was his own, but they had all things in common.

And with great power the Apostles gave witness of the resurrection of the Lord Jesus. And great grace was upon them all.

SPIRITUAL WINNING (EPHESIANS 6:10)

The secret of winning the battles faced in our Christian lives is found in the tenth verse of Ephesians 6. The verse in question says,

Finally, my brethren, be strong in the Lord, and in the power of His might.

The three words used by Paul in this passage are significant.

a. "Be strong" is "endusasthe," in the present passive, imperative, meaning surrender to the Lordship of Jesus Christ and allow His Spirit to empower you!

The word for "supernatural power" is dunamis. That is the basis for the word a*bove that commands believers to surrender to the Lordship of Jesus Christ, whose grace is sufficient for you, just as it was for the apostle Paul. (See 2 Corinthians 12:9.)

b. "Power" is the Greek word *kratos* and means "might or power." "The word refers to strength regarded as abundantly effective in relation to an end to be gained or dominion to be exercised."[33]

c. "Might" is *ischus* and means "strength, strength which one has, power in possession, ability or latent power."[34]

---

[33] Fritz Rienecker and Cleon Rogers, *Linguistic Key to the Greek New Testament* (Zondervan Publishing House), 523–524.
[34] Ibid., 524.

The conclusion of these verbs is that the indwelling Christ and the Holy Spirit enables every believer to experience victorious living, in spite of satanic attacks and his demons who obey his schemes and orders! Our Champion of Love, Jesus, the Son of God, enables all of His children to live godly lives in a world of sin and deceit. Our world is held by Satan in rebellion against the Lord God, but he will be cast into the abyss soon!

1 John 4:4

> Because He who is in you is greater than he who is
> in the world!

An unknown Christian wrote a book titled *How to Live the Victorious Life,* quoted earlier in this work, but here again because he or she has expressed our conclusion perfectly.

> Jesus Christ has won the victory for us. "I live," says
> Paul, "yet not I, Christ liveth in me."
>
> "Ye are of God," says John, "and have overcome
> them." How? Why? "Because greater is He that is
> in you than he that is in the world."
>
> So we come back to the same theme: The secret
> of Victory is in the indwelling Christ. Victory is
> in trusting, not in trying. "This is the victory that
> overcomes the world"—and sin—"even our faith"
> (1 John 5:4).[35]

---

[35] An unknown Christian, *How to Live the Victorious Life* (Grand Rapids, Michigan: Clarion Classics/Zondervan Publishing House, 1986), 23.

The Spiritual Weapons

Chapter 5 has described the illustrations found in the Roman armor. Each item was a word picture of the Captain of our Salvation— our Lord and Savior! The armor of God is not a physical weapon dependent upon the soldier's strength and skillful use of each item!

The panoply of God is spiritual, and each item is an illustration of the founder and finisher of our redemption: "looking unto Jesus, the author and finisher of our faith, who for the joy set before Him endured the cross, despising the shame, and has sat down on the right hand of the throne of God" (Hebrews 6:2).

Consider other passages that define the usage of the whole armor of God.

2 Corinthians 10:3–6

> For though we walk in the flesh, we do not war according to the flesh.
>
> For the weapons of our warfare are not carnal but mighty in God for pulling down strongholds,
>
> Casting down arguments and every high thing that exalts itself against the knowledge of God, bringing every thought into captivity to the obedience of Christ,
>
> And being ready to punish all disobedience is fulfilled.

The passage just quoted is not describing our battle against other people, other denominations, other religions, etc., but we are committed by the Holy Spirit to use the weapons provided for our own sanctification!

1 John 2:15–17

> Do not love the world or the things of the world. If anyone loves the world, the love of the Father is not in him.

> For all that is in the world—the lust of the flesh, the lust of the eyes, and the pride of life—is not of the Father but is of the world.

> And the world is passing away, and the lust of it; but he who does the will of God abides forever.

THE LUST OF THE FLESH

John MacArthur Jr. provides a definition of this expression.

> The lust of the flesh refers to the debased, ignoble cravings of evil hearts. The flesh denotes humanness and its sinful essence. The word translated *lust (epithumia)* is a common New Testament term denoting both positive and negative desires. Here it refers negatively to the sensual impulses from the world that draw people to transgressions. The expression *lust of the flesh* brings to mind primarily sexual sins ...[36]

---

[36] John MacArthur Jr., *The MacArthur New Testament Commentary, 1–3 John* (Chicago, Illinois: Moody Publishers, 2007), 87.

The Lust of the Eyes

When I had the privilege of being on the pastoral team at the Peoples Church in Toronto, I had several appointments with a married couple that was considering separation and divorce. Why? Because the husband was having an affair with a woman he had never met before! What?

Well, the lust of the eyes had captivated this man and had crushed his wife into despair!

In one of our conversations, the husband revealed that his lust driving his affair with another woman than his wife was experienced through his computer and connected to an imaginary female on the internet!

I asked him, "How can you explain your adultery with a blip on a screen? Your lover may be an old woman, a prostitute, or even another man who is creating her from his imagination! You are willing to destroy your marriage so that you can experience sexual lust without a personal or physical contact!"

He was committing "the lust of the eyes!"

There was a pastor in a large church in an American city who was captivated by pornography available through his computer. On a regular basis, he would say to his wife, "I'll be in my study downstairs, but please don't interrupt my research and study. Thanks, dear!"

His study and research were actually "the lust of the eyes" as he spent hours in his study drooling over the naked bodies of models photographed for men!

A survey in the United States discovered that a huge number of pastors, musicians, youth pastors, Sunday school directors, etc. were in bondage to pornography!

Matthew 5:27–28

> Jesus declared,

> You have heard that it was said to those of old, "You shall not commit adultery".

> But I say to you that whoever looks at a woman to lust for her has already committed adultery with her in his heart.

THE PRIDE OF LIFE

Many years ago, I had many conversations with my dad about the condition of the church in general and about the stress, internal arguments, and critical comments. Inevitably, Dad would conclude our discussion by saying, "Son, the biggest sin that we have in our churches is *selfishness!*"

I thought that his statement was too simplistic and needed further research into our "fellowship!" Many years later, I understood that my dad was biblically right and spiritually perceptive.

He was actually describing the Laodicean hypocrisy that is characteristic of today's lukewarm nominal Christians. What we need today is a genuine *brokenness before God and true repentance!*

Norman Grubb

> If God has to deal with us over our impatience or temper in the home, over dishonesty in our business, over coldness or other sins, by no means di we easily bear witness to our brethren of God's faithful and gracious dealings in such areas of failure.

Why not? Just because of pride, self-esteem, although we would often more conveniently call it reserve!

The fact is we love the praise of men as well as of God, and that is exactly what the Scriptures say stops the flow of confession before men (John 12:42–43).[37]

SPIRITUAL WARFARE

The enemy in spiritual warfare is not some other human being! The enemy is not those who belong to another denomination or even those who have no faith in Jesus Christ at all!

Our enemy is the fallen angel called Lucifer and all his demons who are fallen angels. These beings were created as holy angels, but they engaged in "the Luciferian Rebellion." Angels are not human beings that earn a promotion to a higher level, and fallen angels are not fallen human beings that rebelled against God along with Lucifer.

Let's look into the biblical record concerning the fallen most beautiful and powerful archangel.

Satan is mentioned in seven Old Testament books: Genesis, 1 Chronicles, Job (twelve times), Psalms, Isaiah, Ezekiel, and Zechariah.

The New Testament refers to Satan in nineteen books, and every New Testament writer refers to this fallen angel: Matthew 4:1, Mark 5:15, Luke 22:3, 1 John 3:8, Romans 16:20, 1 Peter 5:8, James 4:7, and Jude 9.

---

[37] Norman Grubb, *Continuous Revival* (Fort Washington, Pennsylvania: Christian Literature Crusade, 1971), 16.

The Lord Jesus discussed the reality of Satan some fifteen times: Matthew 4:10, Matthew 16:23, Matthew 25:41, Luke 10:18, John 8:44, John 6:70, and others.

The origin of Satan: Ezekiel 28:12–19 and Isaiah 14:12–14.

The passage in Isaiah contained the fivefold rebellion of this creature.

1. "I will ascend into heaven."
2. "I will exalt my throne above the stars of God."
3. "I will sit upon the mount of the congregation, in the sides of the north."
4. "I will ascend above the heights of the clouds. (Shekinah clouds!)"
5. "I will be like the Most High God."

THE LIMITATIONS OF SATAN

- He is not omnipresent. His secret is that he has millions of demons at his disposal! But Satan is not infinite as God is!
- He is not omnipotent. His power is the greatest of a creature in the universe. He is more powerful than all Christians together, but he cannot overpower a believer in whom the Holy Spirit dwells. The indwelling Christ delivers His children from all of Satan's wiles! (1 John 4:4: "He who is in you is greater than he who is in the world.")
- He is not omniscient. "He knows nothing of God's love, His mercy, His grace, and His forgiveness. The devil does not know the future, nor all the secrets of the past."[38]

---

[38] Dr. H. L Wilmington, *Wilmington's Guide to the Bible* (Wheaton, Illinois: Tyndale House Publishers, Inc.), 769.

THE DEMON POSSESSION/OBSESSION

- Demons are servants to Satan ever since the Luciferian Rebellion. One-third of the holy angels chose to rebel against the Lord God. They became demons forever and will be cast into the abyss called Gehenna. Hell was created by God specifically to punish Satan and all of his fallen angels.
- Demons are given five different terms to describe their area of demonic activity.

  1. *Archai* means "rulers."
  2. *Exousthia* means "authorities."
  3. *Dunameos* means "powers."
  4. *Kureotetos* means "dominions."
  5. *Onomatos* means "names."

Have you ever wondered why gambling is so addictive? Gambling lies in the control of a demon named "Gad!"

Isaiah rebuked the people of Israel who had covenanted with Yahweh that they would never allow another so-called deity to capture their minds, hearts, and wills! They promised to serve and worship Yahweh solely and remain true to Him in all of their lives!

Isaiah 65:11

> But you are those who forsake the Lord, who forget My holy mountain, who prepare a table for Gad and who furnish a drink offering for Meni.

- Gad is the name of a pagan deity known as "Troop" or "Fortune."
- Meni is the name of a pagan deity known as "Number" or "Destiny!"

Yahweh declared His command to His chosen people in a world that was under satanic control!

Isaiah 46:5–9

> To whom will you liken Me, and make Me equal and compare Me, that we should be alike?
>
> They lavish gold out of the bag, and weigh silver on the scales; they hire a goldsmith and he makes a god; they prostrate themselves, yes, they worship.
>
> They bear it on the shoulder, they carry it and set it in its place, and it stands; from its place it shall not move.
>
> Though one cries out to it, yet it cannot answer nor save him out of his trouble.
>
> Remember this, and show yourselves men; recall to mind, O you transgressors,
>
> Remember the former things of old, for I am God, and there is no other; I am God, and there is no other; I am God, and there is none like Me,
>
> Declaring the end from the beginning, and from ancient times things that are not yet done, saying, "My counsel shall stand, and I will do all My pleasure."

The apostle John wrote his Gospel, three epistles, and the book of Revelation. It was this beloved apostle of Christ who wrote, "We know that we are of God, and the whole world lies under the sway of the wicked one" (1 John 5:19).

Notice Revelation 12:7–12.

> And war broke out in heaven: Michael and his angels fought with the dragon; and the dragon and his angels fought,
>
> But they did not prevail, nor was a place found for them in heaven any longer.
>
> So the great dragon was cast out, that serpent of old, called the Devil and Satan, who deceives the whole world; he was cast to the earth, and his angels were cast out with him.
>
> Then I heard a loud voice saying in heaven, "Now salvation, and strength, and the kingdom of our God, and the power of His Christ have come, for the accuser of our brethren, who accused them before our God day and night, has been cast down.
>
> And they overcame him by the blood of the Lamb and by the word of their testimony, and they did not love their lives to the death.
>
> Therefore rejoice, O heavens, and you who dwell in them! Woe to the inhabitants of the earth and the sea! For the devil has come down to you, having great wrath, because he knows that he has a short time.

The Lord answered our prayers in the first church that my wife, Ann, and I served in the town of Leamington, Ontario.

As a student at Toronto Baptist Seminary, I was given the assignment of starting a church in Leamington, and we held our first Sunday morning service on August 4, 1964. We struggled through the first three years, and the Lord provided us with a church building on Elliott Street that had a capacity of 250. Our group of twenty-seven members thought it would be a long time before we could fill the auditorium! But the Lord had other thoughts.

Three years later, I was blessed by training many of our people with Evangelism Explosion, and we took our team to the Leamington District Agricultural Fair in 1969. We established an attractive booth in the corner of the arena floor. Our space was based on seventy-five feet around the curve and was included the seating area behind the curved boards.

In this space, we created a curved backdrop painted with white on the bottom and red on the top, with artificial grass in the middle including white wrought iron lawn furniture. We also created a large screen with a reverse projection of slides of the Holy Land. Instrumental music was also continued playing Gospel music.

In five days, the Lord opened the hearts of 205 people who came in for counseling and received Jesus Christ as Savior and Lord! During the three years including this amazing harvest of souls at the fair, our people were on fire sharing the good news of the grace of God and the gift of eternal life! This little church was blessed with one thousand professions of faith in this short time frame! PTL!

Satan was frustrated with losing the souls of over one thousand new believers! While we were continuing to receive a phenomenal harvest, we suddenly experienced a staggering attack from Satan and his fallen angels!

In four months, Ann and I were confronted with fourteen cases of demonic possession in the lives of people in six towns and cities nearby! Without an exception, each person who wanted deliverance found it by the grace and power of Jesus Christ, our Savior and the Captain of our Salvation!

We all came to understand that a saint indwelt by the Holy Spirit had the power to set sinners from their bondage to Lucifer!

> "You are of God, little children, and have overcome them, because He who is in you is greater than he who is in the world" (1 John 4:4).

SPIRITUAL WALKING

A sinner who was in satanic bondage became a child of the King of kings and Lord of lords in the second of his or her new birth through faith in Jesus alone for salvation (John 1:10–13)!

> He was in the world and the world was made through Him, and the world did not know Him. He came to His own creation(margin), and His own people (margin) did not receive Him. But as many as received Him to them He gave the right (authority—margin) to become the children of God, to those who believe in His Name: who were born, not of blood, nor of the will of the flesh, nor of the will of man, but of God.

No one in the family of God needs to worry or fret about being attacked by Satan and his troops! Because of Calvary and the empty tomb, we are more than conquerors in the name of Jesus Christ!

Romans 8:37

> Yet in all these things we are more than conquerors
> through Him who loved us!

1 Corinthians 15:57

> But thanks be to God, who gives us the victory
> through our Lord Jesus Christ.

1 John 5:4

> For whatever is born of God overcomes the world.
> And this is the victory that has overcome the
> world—our faith!

Victory is not won by the willpower of a human being or from the promises made to God as found in New Year's resolutions!

The secret rests in our relationship with the Lordship of Christ.

The apostle Paul wrote a second letter to the Christians in Corinth in which he asked them a question. "To the one we are the aroma of death leading to death, and to the other the aroma of life leading to life. And who is sufficient for these things?"

Paul then supplies his readers with the answer in chapter 3, verse 5. "Not that we are sufficient of ourselves to think of anything as being of ourselves, but our sufficiency is of God."

Dr. Charles F. Stanley has produced an excellent book of devotions titled *Every Day in His Presence,* and on the page for January 31, he declares,

How will God help you succeed in all you have to do today? He gave you the most important Resource you will ever need when you accepted Jesus as your Savior. It was at that time that the Spirit of God came to indwell you—to teach, prepare, enable, equip energize and empower you for challenges just like the one you face today. He wants to guide you and give you strength. Look for His activity in your life, listen to Him, and obey His promptings.[39]

Galatians 5:16

> I say then, walk in the Spirit and you shall not fulfill the lust of the flesh.

Verse 25 says, "If we live in the Spirit, let us also walk in the Spirit."

"Walk" in verse 16 is *peripate,* which means "to walk, to walk about," and the verb is in the present active imperative meaning that we are to continuously maintain a close fellowship with the Holy Spirit who lives within us.

"Walk" in verse 25 is *stoikomen,* which means "to stand in a row, to walk in a straight line, to behave properly." "The word was used for movement in a definite line, as in a military formation or in dancing."[40]

The message in the usage of these two Greek words is clear. Every Christian has the liberty from sinful habits and the lust of the flesh!

---

[39] Dr. Charles F. Stanley, *Every Day in His Presence:* (Nashville, Tennessee: Thomas Nelson), 36.

[40] Fritz Rienecker and Cleon Rogers, *Linguistic Key to the Greek New Testament* (Grand Rapids, Michigan: The Zondervan Corporation), 518.

The indwelling of the Holy Spirit enables us to claim victory over satanic attacks every moment of every day!

Consider 1 Corinthians 10:13.

> No temptation has overtaken you except such as is common to man; but God is faithful, who will not allow you to be tempted beyond what you are able, but with the temptation will also make the way of escape, that you may be able to bear it.

Jesus clarified this promise in a well-known verse found in John 14:6. "I am the way, the truth, and the life. No one comes to the Father except through Me."

J. HUDSON TAYLOR

The pioneer missionary in the interior of China who had come to full realization of the Savior as the ever-present, indwelling One, testified: "My soul is so happy in the Lord! And as I think of the blessing He gave me on the happy day ... I know not how sufficiently to thank and praise Him. Truly Jesus is the great need of our souls. And He is the great gift of our Father's love—who gave Himself for us, and makes us one with Him in resurrection life and power."

"He is a joyous man now, a bright, happy Christian. He had been a toiling, burdened one before, with latterly not much rest of soul. It was resting in Jesus now, and letting Him do the work—which makes all the difference!" Thus spoke a fellow missionary of Hudson Taylor.[41]

---

[41] V. Raymond Edman, *They Found the Secret* (Grand Rapids, Michigan: Zondervan Publishing House), 17.

ON SPEAKING TERMS

When two people stop speaking to each other, their relationship suffers deeply. In fact, silence can drive the two people apart and even separate husband from wife and teenager from parents.

Some people habitually speak to themselves! Others observe this and conclude that such behavior indicates a mental weakness!

Instead of talking to yourself, you should converse with the indwelling Spirit of the Living God!

Consider the following verses:

Ephesians 6:18–20

> Praying always with all prayer and supplication in the Spirit; being watchful to this end with all perseverance and supplication for all the saints— and for me, that utterance may be given to me, that I may open my mouth boldly to make known the mystery of the gospel, for which I am an ambassador in chains; that in it I may speak boldly, as I ought to speak.

1 Thessalonians 5:17–19

> Pray without ceasing,
> In everything giving thanks; for this is the will of God in Christ Jesus for you.
> Do not quench the Spirit.

2 Corinthians 10:4–6

> For the weapons of our warfare are not carnal but mighty in God for pulling down strongholds,
>
> Casting down arguments and every high thing that exalts itself against the knowledge of God, bringing every thought into captivity to the obedience of Christ,
>
> And being ready to punish all disobedience when your obedience is fulfilled.

This passage is not describing our warfare against other people but the internal battle between the old nature we received at our birth and our new nature (the indwelling Spirit of God) given to us at the new birth (John 3:3–8).

On the other hand, the Lord has equipped us with the panoply of God so that we can win the battles brought into our hearts by Satan and his demons.

Take the time to read this amazing passage.

1 John 3:1–10

> Behold what manner of love the Father has bestowed upon us, that we should be called the children of God! Therefore the world does not know us, because it did not know Him.
>
> Beloved, now we are the children of God; and it has not yet been revealed what we shall be, but we know that when He is revealed, we shall be like Him, for we shall see Him as He is.

And everyone who has this hope in Him purifies himself, just as He is pure.

Whoever commits sin also commits lawlessness, and sin is lawlessness.

And you know that He was manifested to take away our sins, and in Him there is no sin.

Whoever abides in Him does not sin (continues in sin). Whoever sins has neither seen Him nor known Him.

Little children, let no one deceive you; he who practices righteousness is righteous, just as He is righteous.

He who sins (practices sin) is of the devil, for the devil has sinned from the beginning. For this purpose the Son of God was manifested, that He might destroy the works of the devil.

Whoever has been born of God does not sin (practices), for His seed remains in him; and he cannot sin, because he cannot sin, because he has been born of God.

In this the children of God and the children of the devil are manifest: whoever does not practice righteousness is not of God, nor is he who does not love his brother.

2 Corinthians 5:17

Therefore, if anyone is in Christ, he is a new creation; old things have passed away; behold, all things have become new.

The key to victorious Christian living is to talk to Jesus (perhaps silently, if necessary) every moment that you can! Tell Him your struggles and failures. Tell Him your anxieties, worries, frustrations, etc.

Surrender every part of your being to the Lordship of Jesus Christ every day!

2 Corinthians 5:9

> Therefore, we make it our aim, whether present or absent, to be well pleasing to Him.

Ephesians 5:20

> Giving thanks always for all things to God the Father in the Name of our Lord Jesus Christ.

NOTES

- Human beings are not sinners because they sin; they sin because they are sinners!
- Christians are not saints because they are given victory over sin; they are given the victory over sin because they surrender to the Lordship of Jesus every moment of every day! PTL!

Printed in the United States
by Baker & Taylor Publisher Services